Improving Markets for Recycled Plastics

TRENDS, PROSPECTS AND POLICY RESPONSES

OECD
BETTER POLICIES FOR BETTER LIVES

Please cite this publication as:
OECD (2018), *Improving Markets for Recycled Plastics: Trends, Prospects and Policy Responses*, OECD Publishing, Paris.
http://dx.doi.org/10.1787/9789264301016-en

ISBN 978-92-64-30100-9 (print)
ISBN 978-92-64-30101-6 (PDF)

Photo credits: Cover Photo of plastic recycling: © Ulrich Mueller / Shutterstock.com; Arrow adapted from: © Maxim Matsevich / Shutterstock.com

Corrigenda to OECD publications may be found on line at: *www.oecd.org/about/publishing/corrigenda.htm*.

Foreword

Plastics have become one of the most ubiquitous materials in our everyday lives. Their remarkable properties have made them essential in a wide range of sectors, generating a number of benefits for society and for the environment. Plastics are used to protect or preserve foodstuffs, helping to reduce food waste, and to build lighter and more fuel efficient vehicles, helping to reduce greenhouse gas emissions. Plastics are now one of the most important material categories by volume, with global production surpassing that of other key products such as paper and aluminium.

However, the proliferation of plastics has also brought adverse environmental impacts that are associated with their production, use and disposal. The most prominent among these impacts is the increasing amount of the material that can now be found in our oceans. This has disastrous consequences for marine ecosystems, especially with respect to the loss of birds, fish and other wildlife. By mid-century, it is estimated that the ocean could have more plastic than fish by weight. As the fish are eating this plastic it is likely to be ending up in our stomachs, bringing health risks. In addition, plastics are also generating a broad range of environmental challenges, including significant releases of greenhouse gases.

This has sparked strong interest in more efficient production, use and disposal of plastics, in line with the principles of the circular economy. However, plastics recycling rates are still relatively low at between 9 to 30% globally. More needs to be done. The environmental impacts of plastics can be reduced in a number of ways. These include better collection and treatment of waste plastics; the promotion of waste prevention strategies such as the introduction of reusable plastic products; the substitution of alternative, less environmentally harmful materials; the development of bio-based or bio-degradable plastics, or, last but not least, the design of more easily recyclable plastics and effective recovery at end-of-life.

Many governments are now actively working to address this issue and some are developing strategies that specifically focus on plastics, such as the EU's plastics strategy that forms part of its circular economy action plan. The OECD's Environment Policy Committee has made the transition to a circular economy a priority, with a strong focus on plastics. The issue of marine plastics has also been taken up by the G7 under the Canadian Presidency.

Improving Markets for Recycled Plastics: Trends, Prospects and Policy Responses has been developed by the Environmental Policy Committee's Working Party on Resource Productivity and Waste. This study can help to support government efforts to improve plastics recycling in order to increase the amount and the quality of recycled plastics along with the uptake of recycled material in the economy. In particular, it focuses on the barriers that exist within secondary plastics markets and identifies potential interventions that could help to overcome them. On the demand side, policy measures need to focus on helping establish a separate demand for recycled plastics, for instance through the introduction of recycled content labels, and levelling the playing field between virgin and recycled plastics. On the supply side, measures are needed to help increase the volume of recovered plastics and the quality of the resulting feedstock, which requires investment in separate waste collection infrastructure, as well as innovation in product design and processing technologies.

This new study from the OECD can help support the design, development and delivery of policies to make our use of plastics more sustainable, enabling our societies and economies to reap the benefits of plastics, while avoiding associated impacts to the environment, health and to the economy.

Angel Gurría
Secretary General
OECD

Acknowledgements

This report has been developed under the responsibility of the Working Party on Resource Productivity and Waste (WPRPW). It was authored by David Lerpiniere and Ed Cook of Resource Futures. We would also like to thank Roland Geyer at UC Santa Barbara for the important data on plastic production and waste plastics that he provided in the context of this report. Within the OECD Secretariat, the work was managed by Peter Börkey under the overall supervision of Shardul Agrawala, the Head of the Environment and Economy Integration Division. The work was further supported by Andrew McCarthy and Frithjof Laubinger. Laura Dockings and Soojin Jeong provided secretarial support to the project.

Table of contents

Figures

Tables

Boxes

Acronyms and abbreviations

ABS	Acrylonitrile-Butadiene-Styrene
BPA	Bisphenol A
CN	Combined Nomenclature
EP	Epoxide
EPS	Expanded polystyrene
EU	European Union
HS	Harmonised system
HDPE	High Density Polyethylene
HMRC	Her Majesty's Revenue and Customs Authority (UK)
LCA	Lifecycle Assessment
LDPE	Low Density Polyethylene
MDPE	Medium density polyethylene
Mt	Million tonnes
NAFTA	North American Free Trade Agreement
pa	Per Annum
PC	Polycarbonate
PET	Polyethylene Terephthalate
PP	Polypropylene
PP&A	Polyester, polyamide and acrylic
PS	Polystyrene
PU	Polyurethane
PVC	Polyvinyl Chloride
RIM	Reaction Injection Moulded
SITC	Standard International Trade Classification
UN	United Nations
UP	Unsaturated polyester
XLPE	Cross-linked polyethylene

Currency conversions

Where possible, currency has been reported in USD throughout the document. Many of the financials are reported over a large timeframe. Conversion rates are for those reported at the time of writing.

	USD	**CNY**	**EUR**	**GBP**
USD	1	6.46	0.83	0.76
CNY	0.15	1		
EUR	1.21		1	
GBP	1.32			1

Executive summary

Introduction

Plastics are a remarkable family of materials with properties which have allowed them to be applied in a wide range of sectors, including packaging (its most common application by weight), the automotive sector, electronic and electrical equipment, textiles and the construction sector. Global plastics production has risen steeply from modest levels of approximately two million tonnes in the 1950s to approximately 407 million tonnes in 2015.

It is estimated that between 14% and 18% of the waste plastics generated globally are collected for recycling and 24% is incinerated. The remainder is disposed of to landfill, or via open burning, uncontrolled dumping, or is released to the wider environment. There is a vide variation in recycling rates across different polymers, with PET and HDPE (mostly used for packaging) being recycled at relatively high rates (19 to 85%), while PP, PS are much less recycled (1 to 21%). There is also significant disparity in performance across OECD countries, ranging from 30% plastics recycling in the EU to around 10% in the United States.

Uncontrolled waste management is still prevalent in many low and middle income country contexts, where an estimated two billion people are thought not to have access to waste collection services. As such, a substantial quantity of waste plastics is not recycled with a significant proportion of these escaping into the wider environment.

The environmental case for higher recycling rates

A wide range of studies have demonstrated the strong environmental case for recycling rather than landfilling or incinerating plastics. Traditional plastics production is highly energy-intensive, and is estimated to account for 400 million tonnes of greenhouse gas emissions each year (around 1% of the global total in 2012). In addition, the fossil fuel feedstock used in plastics production represents around 4% of global oil and gas production. The hydrocarbon molecules that are bound into the structure of plastics are initially inert, but release greenhouse gases and other pollutants when incinerated.

Mismanaged plastics – those that are disposed of outside organised treatment and disposal systems – also generate significant environmental damage. The proliferation of marine plastics has impacts on ecosystem health, the quality of the coastal environment, and therefore on the viability of the tourism and fisheries industries. The cost of these damages has been estimated at USD 13 billion per annum. In addition, there is some evidence that the ingestion of plastics by fish, and the possible migration of their constituent chemical additives into the food chain, could pose risks to human health.

Open burning of plastics releases harmful pollutants and the escape of plastics into the wider environment has significant negative effects on local communities, ecosystems and economies.

Despite some progress, markets for recycled plastics remain relatively small and vulnerable

Despite a significant increase in the size of markets for recycled plastics, due to a range of policy measures that have supported their development, these markets remain relatively small and exposed to a number of important risks:

- In the market, primary and recycled plastics appear to be treated as substitutes, and the demand for recycled plastics largely results from unsatisfied demand for primary material. There does currently not appear to be a significant separate demand for recycled material, which leaves markets for recycled plastics exposed to trends in primary markets.
- The price of recycled plastics is largely driven by the price of virgin plastics, which in turn is driven by oil prices. This means that the price of recycled plastics is disconnected from the costs that are incurred in producing them, which are mostly driven by the costs of collecting, sorting and processing plastic waste. Producers of recycled plastics are therefore left with few options to adjust their costs in a downturn.
- In comparison to the primary plastics industry, the plastics recycling sector is smaller and more fragmented. The annual throughput and turnover of primary plastics producers is typically about ten times that of the average recycled plastics producer, which puts the sector at a significant disadvantage in terms of the economies of scale that can be exploited and its ability to absorb market shocks, such as the recent collapse in oil prices.
- Finally, much of the global market for plastics waste has been concentrated in a small number of countries. For example, China has accounted for roughly two thirds of waste plastics imports during the last decade. This makes markets for recycled plastics relatively vulnerable and slow to adjust to different types of demand shocks. The import restrictions implemented by China in early 2018 are one such example.

The extent to which markets are exposed to these risks varies according to type of polymer, as markets for some are more developed than for others.

Additional barriers to more effective markets for recycled plastics

In addition to the economic challenges, there are a range of other barriers to the further development of markets for recycled plastics (see Table 0.1):

- **Technical challenges** associated with the wide variety of polymers and additives used, the significant levels of contamination in post-consumer waste plastics, and the practical challenges associated with collecting waste plastics, particularly in low and middle income countries.
- **Environmental challenges** posed by the presence of hazardous additives in some waste plastics, concerns over environmental standards in local recycling industries in some parts of the world, and competition between recycling and energy from waste.

- **Regulatory challenges**, principally associated with illegal waste trade but also due to constraints posed by existing regulation and uncontrolled dumping and burning of wastes, particularly in lower income contexts.

Potential interventions to improve markets

Given the diversity and scale of the challenge facing markets for recycled plastics, a range of measures and interventions will be needed. This will require close partnership working amongst all stakeholders, including policy-makers, regulators, municipalities, industry and communities. Neglecting to engage a key part of the supply chain (e.g. product designers or primary resin producers) could jeopardise the effectiveness of any future policy interventions.

A wide range of potential regulatory, economic, technology, data/information or voluntary interventions could be deployed to address the barriers to properly functioning markets for recycled plastics. As part of this study, key interventions were mapped against the barriers they could address and were considered in terms of three factors: 1) their maturity (i.e. how well-established is the intervention at present); 2) feasibility (i.e. how easy would it be to implement in terms of economic and technical feasibility and stakeholder issues); and 3) what is the potential level of impact (i.e. what barriers could the intervention address?).

The outcome of this qualitative assessment exercise is illustrated in Figure 6.1. In overview, the most promising interventions fall into three groups:

Well-established interventions that have a demonstrated moderate to high impact:

- Setting statutory targets for recycling to drive supply of material, increase economies of scale, reduce costs and increase resilience.
- Using Extended Producer Responsibility (EPR) regulation to drive supply of material and increase economies of scale, reduce costs and increase resilience.
- Raising public awareness to create demand for plastics recycling, reduce contamination and to reduce dumping and uncontrolled dumping.

Interventions that are less well-established but are feasible and have the potential to have a high impact:

- Using public sector procurement policies to create demand for recycled content.
- Sharing best practice on all aspects of the collection, sorting and reprocessing supply chain.
- Developing and sharing market information to allow actors to expand into new markets.
- Providing information and training to designers and manufacturers to encourage use of recycled content.
- Providing information to consumers to encourage purchase of products using recycled content and drive demand.
- Working with supply chain to encourage use of recycled content.

Interventions that are less well-established and are more challenging to implement, but could potentially have a high impact:

- Enforcement action to reduce illegal dumping, particularly in low and middle income countries where dumping is common-place.
- Enforcement action to reduce illegal waste trafficking.
- Mandating requirement for recycled content to create demand.
- Mobilising investment for developing collection, sorting and processing systems, particularly in low income contexts.
- Using financial market mechanisms to increase the resilience of the market to fluctuations in prices (e.g. futures markets or centrally managed risk funds).
- Supporting development of domestic reprocessing capacity to reduce reliance on global markets.
- Using taxes or trading mechanisms to internalise the externalities associated with primary plastics.
- Supporting development of better and more cost-effective technologies for collecting, transporting and sorting waste plastics.
- Supporting the development and demonstration of commercially viable technologies for reprocessing mixed and/or low value plastics.
- Mandating requirement for recycled content to create demand.
- Industry-led initiative to standardise polymers and additives, and improve information on additives.
- Industry-led initiatives to crack down on waste crime.

Overall, no single intervention represents a solution. The creation of properly functioning markets for recycled plastics will require action at global, national and local levels.

Table 0.1. **Summary of barriers to better functioning markets for recycled plastics**

No	Barrier	Summary
Economic barriers		
1	**Costs of collecting, sorting and processing waste plastics are high**	This is due to the widely distributed and diverse nature of sources of plastics waste; the combination of polymers of different types and with other materials within products; and high levels of contamination of post-consumer plastics.
2	**Limited resilience of the sector to market shock.**	The recycling industry is characterised by many small-scale operators who are unable to withstand decreases in market prices. This issue is further compounded by a recycling sector that has limited control over the quality of its inputs and over demand for its products.
3	**Global markets concentrated in a small number of countries**	The concentration of demand for recovered plastics in a small number of countries renders the market vulnerable to demand shocks. The emerging effects of the import restrictions implemented by China in early 2018 provide an example of the implications of this market concentration.".
4	**Lack of differentiated demand for recycled plastics.**	Recycled plastics are generally treated as a replacement material for primary plastics. Although demand for recycled plastics is influential in the short term, it is the price of oil and primary plastics price that drive recycled plastics market prices over the long term.
5	**Poor data on the structure and performance of the sector**	Poor data on the plastics recycling sector limits the extent to which market actors can make evidence-based decisions and dissuades new market entrants.

Table 0.1. **Summary of barriers to better functioning markets for recycled plastics** *(continued)*

No	Barrier	Summary
Technical barriers		
1	**Collection systems for wastes are not available for a substantial proportion of the global population**	An estimated two billion people globally do not have access to waste collection services which means a substantial proportion of global plastics waste are being burnt in the open or are escaping into the wider environment.
2	**Waste plastics are often contaminated and mixed with other materials**	Contamination of post-consumer waste plastics is high, necessitating removal using appropriate equipment. Also, identifying and successfully separating polymers that are mixed together in the waste stream is technically challenging, and the very large number of different types of polymer and additives used also increases the challenge.
3	**Problematic additives**	Some additives used in primary plastics can have a detrimental effect on the physical characteristics of recycled plastics (for example, affecting brittleness, flame retardancy and oxidation). A critical issue is that of degradability enhancers which can significantly affect the strength and durability of recycled plastics and, if they were to become widespread in primary plastics would potentially prevent plastics recycling entirely. The issue is compounded by the lack of transparency around the presence and nature of additives that may be present in primary plastics.
4	**Biodegradable plastics mixing with other plastics.**	Biodegradable plastics cannot be recycled using conventional mechanical recycling techniques. Some biodegradable plastics are easily mistaken for and mixed with conventional plastics, contaminating both recyclate streams and biological treatment facilities alike.
5	**Limited collection schemes and treatment technologies for thermosets**	Collection systems and treatment technologies for thermosets are not well-established and are thought to be limited to commercial and industrial sources, and some specific items that arise in the municipal waste (e.g. household appliances).
Environmental barriers		
1	**Hazardous additives.**	Hazardous additives used in primary plastics can make their way into recycled plastics where they may pose a health risk, particularly where they are present in products that are used for sensitive applications such as toys and food packaging. This concern is compounded by the lack of transparency in the use of additives in plastics.
2	**Competition between recycling and energy from waste.**	There is a risk that, in specific contexts, energy-from-waste will compete for access to waste plastics as a feedstock thus pushing plastics towards a less-preferred option in environmental terms. Due to the typically long-term contracts associated with energy from waste infrastructure, there is a risk of long-term "lock-in" should local or national governments chose to establish energy from waste as a means to manage waste plastics. This could limit investment in recycling infrastructure in the short term.
3	**Concerns over environmental standards for recycling in emerging markets.**	Concerns about relatively weak environmental standards may lead to restrictions on the flow of plastics waste (and derivatives) to jurisdictions where recycling costs are the lowest.
Regulatory barriers		
1	**Regulatory burden of materials classified as waste**	Regulatory requirements that affect materials classified as a "waste" can create additional costs for recyclers and also reduce the perceived value of the recycled material.
2	**Illegal trafficking in waste plastics.**	The illegal waste trade is estimated at USD 10-12 billion annually. This has a significant effect on plastics trade as it undermines the quality of compliant material.
3	**Uncontrolled dumping and burning of municipal wastes.**	Poor enforcement against illegal disposal of wastes can undermine the market for recycled plastics.

Chapter 1

Introduction

This chapter sets out the motivation for the development of this report. It highlights the rapid growth in plastics production and use that has taken place in recent decades, and notes the increase in plastic waste generation and pollution that has occurred as a consequence. The risks associated with continued business as usual growth in plastics use are then discussed, and improved waste collection and recycling systems are identified as a key means of addressing the problem. The chapter concludes by highlighting the role that stronger and more stable markets for waste and recycled plastics could play in boosting recycling rates.

1.1. The growth in plastics

Plastics are fast becoming one of the most prolific materials on the planet. Half of all the plastics ever produced were made in the last 13 years (Geyer, Jambeck and Law, 2017[1]). The term "plastics" encompasses a wide range of material types which are prized for their high strength to weight ratio, versatility, and resistance to chemical, biological and physical degradation. These properties have led to plastics being used as a substitute for materials such as concrete, glass, metals, wood and paper.

However, the pervasiveness of plastics has not been without its drawbacks. Plastics use approximately 4% by mass of all oil extracted as a raw material (Hopewell, Dvorak and Kosior, 2009[2]). Their production and use emits approximately 400 million tonnes of greenhouse gas (GHG) emissions annually (European Commission, 2017[3]) as a result of the energy used in refinement and production, transport to the user, and waste treatment or disposal.

Conversely, the lightness and durability of plastics can reduce transport emissions when compared to other heavier or less durable materials. A Plastics Europe report (2010[4]) found that using alternatives to plastics could increase the mass of packaging by a factor of 3.6 and therefore greenhouse gas emissions by a factor of 2.6. Furthermore, plastics are often used to protect or preserve other products such as food and through doing so, reduce associated wastage.

1.2. Plastics waste

Where waste plastics enter the formal waste management system, they are either recycled, or disposed of in controlled landfill or incinerators (which may or may not recover electricity, heat or by-products). However, in communities where formal waste management systems do not exist, particularly in informal communities in low and middle-income countries, a substantial proportion of waste plastics are disposed of in uncontrolled dumps, watercourses, or burned openly (UNEP, 2016[4]).

Plastics disposed of in landfills break down over many hundreds of years, slowly emitting methane in the process. The same process takes place when plastics are disposed of in the natural environment, albeit at slower rates and with carbon dioxide as the by-product. In both cases, the environmental impact is often underestimated because of the timescales involved.

Thermal decomposition, either controlled or uncontrolled, also results in GHG emissions. If energy is recovered, as in some incineration, gasification or pyrolysis facilities, the overall emissions may be slightly lower than a direct fossil source (i.e. coal, gas or oil), because the material has already had a use and the alternative may be disposal as discussed above.

Material which has been disposed of into watercourses has a range of detrimental effects on the aquatic life, including bioaccumulation, chemical leaching, prevention of transfer of oxygen and nutrients in the benthic zone (USEPA, 2011[6]).[1] All of the world's major ocean basins have been found to contain plastic debris (Barnes et al., 2009[5]) and it has been estimated that between 4 and 12 Mt entered the oceans in 2010 (Jambeck et al., 2015[6]).

1.3. Plastics recycling

If recent trends continue, an estimated 26 billion tonnes of plastics will be produced over the next ~30 years (Geyer, Jambeck and Law, 2017[1]). The environmental burden associated with the production, use, and eventual disposal of these plastics will tend to increase in parallel. Reducing these burdens will require greater efficiency of plastics use. This will require a change in thinking from traditional linear economic models (i.e. manufacture-use-dispose), to more circular economic models, whereby the use of plastics is optimised (e.g. through product redesign and light-weighting),[2] and plastics are kept within the use cycle for longer, through reuse and recycling. Other management routes for waste plastics, such as reuse or thermal treatment with energy recovery, may be preferable to recycling in certain contexts, but increased recycling of plastics is still likely to be an essential part of a circular economy transition.

Recycling of waste plastics emerged during the early 1990s. Since that time, the global rate of recycling has increased by approximately 0.7% per annum to the current rate of 20% (Geyer, Jambeck and Law, 2017[1]). Recycling rates for waste plastics differ significantly between different polymers, applications and regions. Packaging plastics, and the polymers commonly used in packaging (e.g. PET, HDPE and LDPE), represent the majority of plastics that are collected for recycling. Recycling rates for plastics from other sectors, such as automotive, construction, and electrical equipment, and for other polymers, are substantially lower. Europe has the highest recycling rate for plastics, followed by Japan and North America. Very little data is available on recycling rates in other countries, but it is clear that the informal sector often plays a relatively important role in low and middle income countries.

Recycling rates for materials such as aluminium (~50%) (International Aluminium Institute, 2013[7]) and paper (~43%) (UPM, 2016[8]) are significantly higher than those for plastics. This is partly a consequence of the relative maturity and economic attractiveness of metal and paper recycling, but also results from a number of technical issues associated with recycling of plastics. These include the presence of problematic and/or hazardous additives, separation techniques, efficient transport and removal of contamination at source. Furthermore, recycled plastics differ from materials such as metals, in that the properties that make them attractive such as durability and lightness, reduce each time they are recycled, requiring more material to be used for recycled versus virgin materials.

These challenges have been compounded by weak and unstable global markets for recycled plastics that have resulted in uncertainty and complete market failure at times (WRAP, 2017[9]).[3] The recycled plastics industry is, unlike the primary plastics sector, characterised by numerous small actors, and is therefore vulnerable to any price volatility. Strong and stable markets for recycled plastics will be essential for allowing these barriers to be overcome and driving sustainable growth in plastics recycling as part of a more circular economy.

1.4. Objectives of the report

The aim of this report is to provide a better understanding of the barriers that exist within markets for recycled plastics, and to identify potential interventions that could help enhance and stabilise these markets. This report does not examine secondary plastics reuse markets.

The data presented in this report is based upon a review of data provided by respondents to an OECD questionnaire issued in early 2017. In addition, numerous other sources of data and information have been sought to supplement the information provided in the questionnaires.

This report is structured as follows. Chapter 2 provides an overview of primary plastics production, including the quantities and types produced and the key sectors where it is used. Chapter 3 discusses the environmental case for recycling plastics and presents a snapshot of current plastics generation and recycling rates. Chapter 4 describes the structure of the recycled plastics industry. Chapter 5 discusses markets and trade in waste plastics. Chapter 6 discusses the key barriers to the efficient functioning of markets for recycled plastics and considers the range of potential interventions that could be used to help markets function more effectively. Supporting information is provided in annexes.

Notes

1. The benthic zone is the ecological region at the lowest level of a body of water such as an ocean or a lake, including the sediment surface and some sub-surface layers.
2. Light-weighting is the term that describes when manufacturers produce a product which serves the same purpose, with less weight of material.
3. The fall in plastics prices following the 2007/8 financial crisis saw a reduction of prices for plastics waste to zero or negative figures in some cases.

References

Barnes, D. et al. (2009), "Accumulation and fragmentation of plastic debris in global environments", *Philosophical Transactions of The Royal Society B*, http://dx.doi.org/10.1098/rstb.2008.0205. [5]

European Union((n.d.)), *PolyStyreneLoop Project*, https://circulareconomy.europa.eu/platform/en/good-practices/polystyreneloop-project-pioneer-demonstration-plant-treat-3300-tonnes-polystyrene-wasteyr-2018 (accessed on 26 March 2018). [75]

Geyer, R., J. Jambeck and K. Law (2017), "Production, use, and fate of all plastics ever made", *Science Advances*, Vol. 3/7, p. e1700782, http://dx.doi.org/10.1126/sciadv.1700782. [1]

Hopewell, J., R. Dvorak and E. Kosior (2009), "Plastics recycling: challenges and opportunities.", *Philosophical transactions of the Royal Society of London. Series B, Biological sciences*, Vol. 364/1526, pp. 2115-26, http://dx.doi.org/10.1098/rstb.2008.0311. [2]

International Aluminium Institute (2013), "Global Aluminium Recycling: A Cornerstone of Sustainable Development", www.world-aluminium.org (accessed on 26 March 2018). [7]

Jambeck, J. et al. (2015), "Plastic waste inputs from land into the ocean", https://www.iswa.org/fileadmin/user_upload/Calendar_2011_03_AMERICANA/Science-2015-Jambeck-768-71__2_.pdf (accessed on 28 March 2018). [6]

Plastics Europe (2016), "Plastics – the Facts 2017: An analysis of European plastics production, demand and waste data", https://www.plasticseurope.org/application/files/5715/1717/4180/Plastics_the_facts_2017_FINAL_for_website_one_page.pdf (accessed on 26 March 2018). [17]

U.S. Environmental Protection Agency (2011), *Marine Debris in the North Pacific*, https://nepis.epa.gov/Exe/ZyNET.exe/P100CYAN.TXT?ZyActionD=ZyDocument&Client=EPA&Index=2011+Thru+2015&Docs=&Query=&Time=&EndTime=&SearchMethod=1&TocRestrict=n&Toc=&TocEntry=&QField=&QFieldYear=&QFieldMonth=&QFieldDay=&IntQFieldOp=0&ExtQFieldOp=0&XmlQuery= (accessed on 23 March 2018). [88]

UNEP (2016), *Global Waste Management Outlook*, http://web.unep.org/ourplanet/september-2015/unep-publications/global-waste-management-outlook// (accessed on 27 March 2018). [4]

UPM (2016), "Print and Paper: The Facts", http://assets-upmpaper.upm.com/Shared%20Documents/responsibility/Paper%20is%20one%20of%20the%20most%20recycled%20products.pdf (accessed on 26 March 2018). [8]

WRAP (2017), *Materials Pricing Report*, www.wrap.org.uk/content/materials-pricing-report (accessed on 26 March 2018). [9]

Chapter 2

Plastics production

This chapter summarises current patterns of plastics production, the structure of markets for primary plastics, and the different types of plastics that are produced. It highlights the rapid growth in the production and use of plastics during the last half century, and describes the current distribution of production across different regions. The most widely produced polymers of plastic are also introduced, along with their key characteristics and main sectoral applications. Finally, this chapter concludes with a discussion of bio-based and biodegradable plastics, and the opportunities and risks that these present.

2.1. Primary plastics: production data

Global plastics production increased from around 2 Mtpa in the 1950s to 407 Mtpa in 2015. During that period, it is estimated that 8 300 Mt of plastics have been produced, and of this, around 6 300 Mt are thought to have become waste (Geyer, Jambeck and Law, 2017[1]).

At present, the main regional producers of primary plastics are the Peoples Republic of China, Europe, and North America (see Figure 2.1). Plastics production has grown steadily in China and other parts of Asia over the past decade. Production in Europe and North America dropped during 2008/09 following the economic crisis but has slowly returned to growth, although it is only now reaching pre-economic crisis levels of production.

Figure 2.1. **Plastics production mass by global region in 2016**

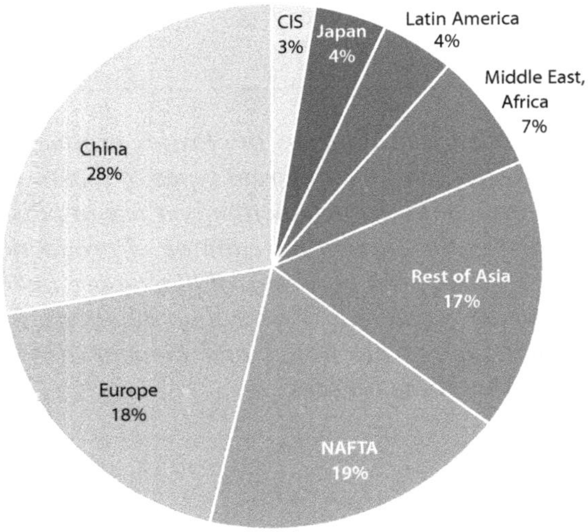

Note: NAFTA: North American Free Trade Agreement; CIS: Commonwealth of Independent States (comprised of former Soviet Union countries).

Source: Plastics Europe (2016[10]) *Plastics – the Facts 2017: An analysis of European plastics production, demand and waste data*, https://bit.ly/2GvymZS.

Plastics are a remarkable family of materials with properties which have allowed them to be applied in a wide range of sectors. The most common use of plastics is as a packaging material, where their light weight and ease of formation into different shapes has made them an essential element of our current systems of transporting and handling products of all types (particularly food and drink items where they have been central in a change from reusable to single-use containers). However, plastics are also widely used in a range of other sectors including the automotive sector, electrical and electronic equipment, textiles and the construction sector. Figure 2.2 shows the global growth in plastics consumption and the sectors where it is used.

Figure 2.2. **Global primary plastics production by sector, 1950 to 2015 (million tonnes)**

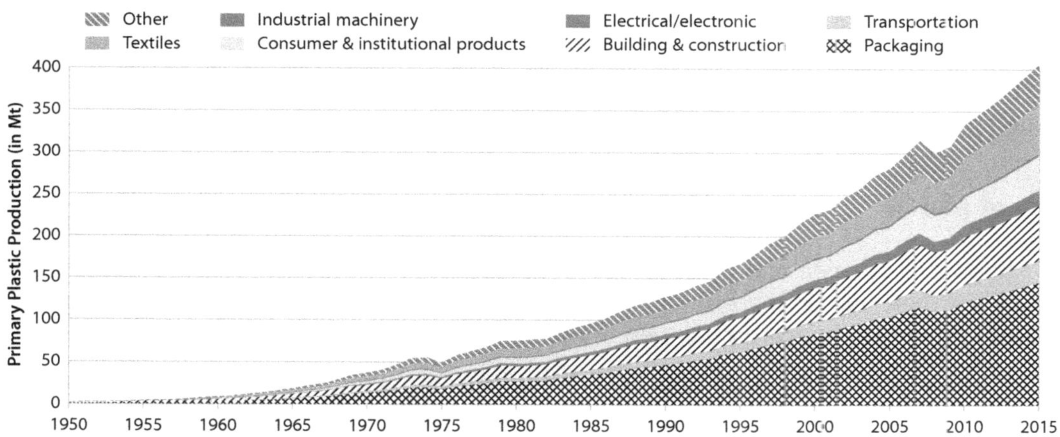

Source: Geyer, Jambeck and Law (2017[1]), *Production, use, and fate of all plastics ever made*, http://bit.ly/2uBs8AT.

2.2. Primary plastics: market structure

Primary plastics production refines crude oil, produces monomers which are then polymerised, and blended into plastics starting materials (see process flow in Annex A).[1] Monomer production is the domain of much larger, mainly oil and chemical companies, which may also carry out polymerisation and blending activities. Other companies will purchase base monomers from those larger companies and polymerise materials on a smaller scale.

The global industry is dominated by a handful of multinational corporations including (total sales value in brackets): Dow Chemical (USD 49 billion); Lyondell Basell (USD 33 billion); Exxon Mobil (USD 236 billion); SABIC (USD 35.4 billion); INEOS (USD 40 billion); BASF (USD 63.7 billion); ENI (USD 61.6 billion); LG Chem (USD 17.8 billion); Chevron Phillips (USD 13.4 billion); and Lanxess (USD 7.9 billion) (Crow, 2016[10]).

Table 2.1. **Summary of UK primary polymer market**

Company	Capacity (tpa)	Polymers produced
Sabic UK	400 000	LDPE
Lotte Chemical	350 000	PET
Inovyn	300 000	PVC
NEOS	285 000	HDPE, LLDPE LDPE
Basell Poleolefins	230 000	PP
Indorama Polymers	168 000	PET
Vinnolt	45 000	PVC
PET Processors (UK) LLC	20 000	PET
Victrex Plc	7 000	Polyetheretherketone (PEEK)
Lucite	3 000	Polymethyl Methacrylate(PMMA)
Asahi Glass Fluoropolymers UK Ltd	3 000	PTFE

Source: British Plastics Federation (2016[12]), *The UK Plastics Industry: A Strategic Vision for Growth*, http://bit.ly/2yfutkx.

At a national level, plastics producers vary in size in terms of throughput as shown in Table 2.1. Whilst some companies have an annual capacity similar to recycled plastics processors, these companies tend to be producing specialist plastics such as PTFE or PEEK. When it comes to the most commonly used materials such as LDPE, HDPE, and PET, the throughputs are around ten times greater than those of the UK recycled plastics re-processors (see Section 4.4).

2.3. Types of plastic

Plastics production and consumption is complex, with a number of stages between the creation of monomers from fossil fuels and their use as a "starting material" for products made of plastics. Annex A presents an overview of the key stages in plastics production and processing.

Plastics can be divided into two broad subsets, thermoplastics and thermosets. Table 2.2 shows some of the most commonly used plastics and some examples of their uses. Table 2.3 provides an overview of the main uses of different polymers by sector.

Table 2.2. **Main types of plastic and their uses**

	Type	Resin ID code	Common uses
Thermoplastics	Polyethylene Terephthalate (PET)	#1	Bottles, textiles, carpets and food packaging (also known as polyester (PE) in the textile industry)
	High-Density Polyethylene (HDPE)	#2	Bottles for detergents, food products, pipes and toys
	Polyvinyl Chloride (PVC)	#3	Window frames, flooring, pipes, wallpaper, bottles, medical products
	Low-Density Polyethylene (LDPE)	#4	Cling-film, bin liners and flexible containers
	Polypropylene (PP)	#5	Yoghurt and margarine pots, auto motive parts, fibres, milk crates
	Polystyrene (PS)	#6	Food containers, egg cartons, plastic picnic cutlery, foam packaging, rigid foam insulation
	Others including polycarbonate, LEXAN and bioplastics	#7	Various uses
Thermosets	Unsaturated polyester (UP)	n/a	Sheet moulding compound, bulk moulding compound and the toner of laser printers – fibreglass reinforced plastics
	Polyurethane (PU)		Coatings, finishes, mattresses and vehicle seating
	Epoxide (EP)		Adhesives, sports equipment, electrical and automotive components
	Phenolic resins (phenoplasts)		Ovens, toaster, automotive parts and circuit boards

Table 2.3. **Summary of estimated global polymer consumption by sector (2002-14)**

Market sector	LDPE, LLDPE	HDPE	PP	PS	PVC	PET	PU	Other	Total
Transportation	0.1%	0.8%	2.6%	0.0%	0.3%	0.0%	1.6%	1.4%	6.7%
Packaging	13.5%	9.3%	8.2%	2.3%	0.9%	10.1%	0.2%	0.1%	44.8%
Building and construction	1.1%	3.3%	1.2%	2.2%	8.1%	0.0%	2.4%	0.5%	18.8%
Electrical/Electronic	0.5%	0.2%	0.9%	0.6%	0.4%	0.0%	0.4%	1.0%	3.8%
Consumer & institutional products	2.9%	1.7%	3.8%	1.8%	0.6%	0.0%	1.0%	0.2%	11.9%
Industrial machinery	0.2%	0.1%	0.2%	0.0%	0.0%	0.0%	0.3%	0.0%	0.8%
Other	1.7%	0.9%	4.2%	0.7%	1.4%	0.0%	2.5%	1.7%	13.2%
Total	**20.0%**	**16.3%**	**21.0%**	**7.6%**	**11.8%**	**10.2%**	**8.2%**	**4.9%**	**100.0%**

Source: Geyer, Jambeck and Law (2017[1]), *Production, use, and fate of all plastics ever made*, http://bit.ly/2uBs8AT.

2.3.1. Thermoplastics

Thermoplastics account for approximately 91% of the mass of plastics produced (CISION, 2015[11]).[2] They differ from thermosets in that they remain chemically stable over a large range of temperatures and can be melted and reshaped into new objects. The main processes used in manufacturing are injection moulding, compression moulding, calendaring, and extrusion.

2.3.2. Thermosets

Thermosets are crosslinked polymers structured in a grid, and are characterised by their high resistance to mechanical force, chemicals, wear and heat. The robust properties of thermosets make them more difficult to recycle and they cannot be re-melted down and reformed like thermoplastics.

The manufacturing methods are similar to thermoplastics but the crosslinking of the polymers tends to take place once the materials have entered in the desired shape via a catalyst (like glue with a hardener).

2.3.3. Additives

Plastics polymers are also combined with a wide range of additives to improve specific properties such as UV, biodegradation, heat, oxidation and acid resistance; flame formation resistance; optical brightness and colour; anti-fogging and anti-static; and resistance to impact. The content of additives in plastics varies widely, from less than 1% in PET bottles and up to 50-60% in PVC (Table 2.4). Often a balance needs to be struck between technical properties and economics, as some additives are considerably more expensive than the main polymers. However, others are inexpensive (e.g. inorganic fillers such as limestone or talc).

There are many thousands of additives which may be added to plastics, several hundred of which are in common use. Most fillers, and a third of flame retardants, are mineral based. A priori data suggest that the majority do not impact on the environment or human health, as they either do not migrate easily from host polymer or do not exhibit toxicity (Galloway, 2015[12]; COWI, 2013[13])

Table 2.4. **Additive use in polymers**

Additive	% weight of the polymer present
Stabilisers	Up to 4%
Plasticisers	Present in flexible PVC at levels of 20-60%
Mineral flame retardants	In soft PVC cables, insulation and sheathing from 5-30%
Fillers	Typically calcium carbonate is present in PVC flooring at very high proportions (50%) and in pipes from 0-30% or more. Talc and glass fibres are used in PP for automotive applications, typically in the range of 20-40%. Glass fibres are also found in engineering polymers (such as PA or PBT), for reinforcement in the range 5-70%
Pigments	Titanium dioxide is present in window profiles at 4-8%

Source: Villanueva and Eder (2014[14]), *End-of-waste criteria for waste plastic for conversion*, http://bit.ly/1y7ADLM.

However, several substances such as bisphenol A (BPA); brominated flame retardants; phthalates; and cadmium/barium and lead stabilisers have been the subject of controversy due to health concerns. Recent scientific evidence has led to some additives being banned in certain applications, and the subject of plastics additives is often treated with broad brush suspicion which is exacerbated by industry's reluctance to publicly share the details of additives used in its products due to commercial sensitivity.

The majority of additives are not altered, consumed or degraded during mechanical recycling as they are resistant to the temperatures applied. Their presence does not normally negatively affect the properties of the recycled plastics. In fact, compatibilisers may aid the mixing of two different polymer types. However, some additives may significantly alter the properties of recycled plastics (e.g. temperature sensitivity, oxidation and brittleness) compared with virgin material. In some cases, this can be overcome with purification steps such as melt filtration, surfactant and solvent washing or with the use of stabilisers to counteract their effects. However, these processes add cost to operations and thus reduce the competitiveness of recycled plastics (Villanueva and Eder, 2014[14]).

Technical barrier: Some additives used in primary plastics affect the physical properties of recycled plastics. A critical issue is that of degradability enhancers. These additives can significantly affect the strength and durability of recycled plastics. Uncertainty around the presence and nature of additives that may be present in primary plastics can dis-incentivise plastics recycling.

Whilst many of the additives used in primary plastics are tightly bound into the host polymer, some smaller molecules are able to migrate to the surface and potentially into humans or the environment. The potential exposure posed by these materials is of particular concern where they are incorporated into recycled plastics and used for applications involving human exposure (e.g. children's toys and food packaging) or where they could be released into the wider environment (e.g. through marine litter). This issue also raises health concerns for workers in the recycling sector. For instance, phthalates (Pivnenko et al., 2016[15]) and brominated flame retardants (DiGangi and Strakova, 2015[16]) have been found in samples of recycled plastics where they would not be expected.

Whilst some of these additives have been phased out by the industry, many are still being produced and/or remain in stock; particularly PVC products which are mainly used in construction and typically have a much longer life time than other plastic products.

A special case is constituted by additives that enhance degradability and that are typically found in bio-degradable plastics. They are a particular threat to plastics re-processors as they inherently reduce the strength and durability of recycled plastics.[3] Their inclusion throughout the market could theoretically end the recycled plastics market if they were applied throughout primary production unless suitable agents could be found to reverse the degradability process, or if such plastics products could be effectively separated from conventional plastics.

Degradability enhancers can also aid the release of other additives into the wider environment. If these additives are dangerous, then this poses a potentially significant human health and environmental risk. Furthermore, degradability enhancers increase the rate at which plastics break into smaller particles once they escape into the environment, allowing them to disperse and impact on ecosystems.

One related, more general concern with additives is the lack of transparency and information about what additives are being used in different materials. This may reduce the appeal of recycled plastics use in products, especially those where they may be absorbed by humans such as baby products or food packaging. The impact on manual workers in plastics sorting facilities is also an area of concern.

Environmental barrier: Hazardous additives used in primary plastics can make their way into recycled plastics where they may pose a health risk, particularly where they are present in products that are used for sensitive applications such as toys and food packaging. This concern is compounded by the lack of transparency in the use of additives in plastics.

A more detailed discussion on the properties of the main additive types and their potential impacts on the market for recycled plastics is provided in Annex B.

2.3.4. Bio-plastics

The term "bio-plastics" encompasses two broad concepts (Plastics Europe, $2016_{[17]}$):

- **Biodegradable plastics** are materials that can be broken down by microorganisms to form water and carbon dioxide (aerobic conditions) or water and methane (anaerobic conditions). They can be produced from either biogenic or fossil carbon sources.
- **Bio-based plastics** are made from contemporary biological sources such as sugar cane, beet sugar, corn, potatoes, grains or vegetable oils. These plastics are not necessarily biodegradable.

Bio-plastics have only recently emerged in the waste stream, but are now gaining a small foothold in the overall polymer industry. There are roughly 21 types of bio-plastic polymers in the marketplace or under development (see Annex C), ten of which are summarised in Table 2.5. As illustrated in Figure 2.3, there is considerable overlap between bio-based plastics and biodegradable plastics. Not all bio-based plastics are biodegradable and some fossil-based plastics are biodegradable.

Table 2.5. **Examples of key bio-plastics**

Polymer	Abv.	Qualities/Applications	Biodegradable	Recycled today	Other notes
Bio-based					
Polyhydroxyalkanoates Polyhydroxybutyrate Poly (3-hydroxybutyrate-co-3-hydroxyvalerate)	PHA PHB PHBV	Can be used as films. PHA can be processed on conventional processing equipment, is UV stable and has potential for medical and pharma. PHB is similar to PP and has good resistance to moisture and aroma barrier properties. PHBV is less stiff and tougher than PHA and may be used as packaging material.	Yes	No	Pilot scale/ High cost today Inherently difficult to scale
Polylactic acid	PLA	Widespread utility, can be processed into fibre or film. Similar mechanical properties to PET. Not UV stable. Can be 3D printed.	Can biodegrade under the right conditions	Yes*	Commercial scale High cost today
Poly-gamma=-butyrolactone	Poly (GBL)	Alternative to PP, with potential applications in packaging, as film, for utensils or medical uses.	Yes	Yes	Only lab scale currently
"Green" adhesives		Non-toxic. Water-soluble.	Yes	No	Current cost; scalability
Old economy bioplastics (rubber, gelatine, cellulose and linoleum)			Yes	Some	
Fossil derived biodegradable					
Polybutyrate	PBAT	Alternative to LDPE and good for plastic bags and wraps due to flexibility and resilience.	Yes	No	High relative cost today
Polycaprolactone	PCL	Limited mechanical properties (impact resistance, brittleness, etc.).FDA-approved for biomedical.	Yes, but more slowly**	No	High relative cost
Polybutylene succinate	PBS	Alternative to PP, with potential applications in packaging, as film, for utensils or medical uses.	Yes	No	High relative cost
Polyglycolide	PGA	Approved for biomedical uses such as dissolving sutures and implantable devices.	Yes	No	

* One company (Looplife Polymers) in Belgium is known to recycle PLA.

** Although PCL is fully biodegradable, its structure is more crystalline than other polymers in its class and therefore it will degrade more slowly.

Source: Moss, Eidson and Jambeck (2017[18]), *Sea of Opportunity: Supply Chain Investment Opportunities to Address Marine Plastic Pollution,* http://bit.ly/2pxLHVf.

2.2.4.1. Bio-based plastics

Some bio-based plastics have identical chemistry to fossil-fuel derived plastics. They are sometimes described as "drop in" plastics because they can be both substituted and mixed with their fossil derived equivalents in existing production lines. Examples include PET, PP, and PE. The benefit of theses drop-in plastics is that they can also be recycled. Conversely, they do not biodegrade. Most other bioplastics are biodegradable but cannot be substituted for conventional fossil-derived (other than possibly Poly–(γ-butyrolactone) (poly (GBL)).

Figure 2.3. **Recyclability and biodegradability of fossil fuel- and bio-based plastics**

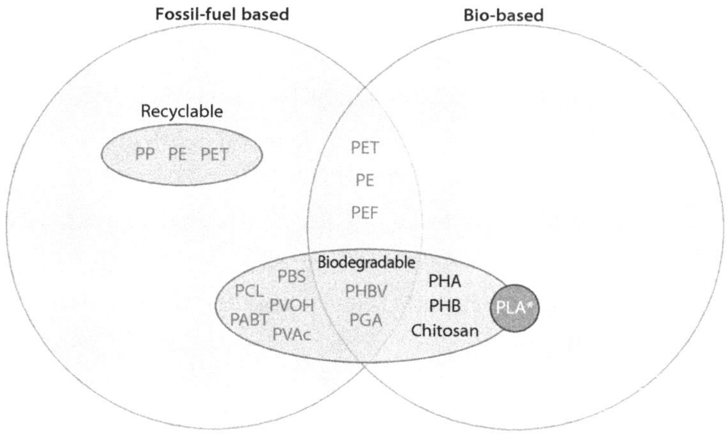

* PLA is only biodegradable in conditions that allow hydrolysis, like industrial composting for example.

Source: Moss, Eidson and Jambeck (2017[20]), *Sea of Opportunity: Supply Chain Investment Opportunities to Address Marine Plastic Pollution,* http://bit.ly/2pxLHVf.

2.2.4.2. Biodegradability

All plastics are thought to be biodegradable given appropriate conditions and sufficient time. However, in the natural environment, most commonly used polymers only biodegrade over periods of tens or even hundreds of years. This means that empirical evidence for the biodegradation of plastics is limited, and that the long-term fate of plastics is largely unknown. It is worth noting that, although most fossil fuel- and bio-based plastics are considered to be biodegradable, a number of important polymers – PET and PE for example – are not (Table 2.5). Annex D provides further information on the definition of different types of degradation.

In this context, it is also important to recognise the distinction between degradability and biodegradability. Plastics that are biodegradable can be broken down by micro-organisms into water and carbon dioxide. Degradability, of which biodegradability is a subset, also includes degradation via other mechanisms such as oxo-degradation (exposure to oxygen) and photo degradation (exposure to sunlight). It is not clear whether plastics that degrade in this way degrade into benign compounds, such as water and carbon dioxide, or whether they just fragment into smaller and smaller particles over time.

Claims about biodegradability should therefore be qualified with:

- a timeframe under which biodegradation can take place;
- a specified set of conditions; and
- the extent to which the material is no longer in its previous form.

There are a number of biodegradability standards that define testing methods for biodegradability and thresholds for defining whether a plastic is "biodegradable" or not.[4] However, at present there are no comprehensive, globally agreed standards on biodegradability as a whole (European Bioplastics, 2016[18]). There is considerable confusion over the conditions and time required for "biodegradable" plastics to degrade and also the substances that are produced by their degradation (e.g. benign, organic compounds or very small fragments of the original material).

For example, two separate compostability standards for packaging have been applied in Europe (EN13432), and the US (ASTM D400 and D6868). There is also a related international standard for compostable plastics (ISO 17088), which also covers non-packaging. Although the standards differ to some extent, they include the following broad definitions for compostable plastics (Michaud, Farrant and Jan, 2010[19]):

- **Chemical characteristics**: it contains at least 50% organic matter (based on dry weight) and does not exceed a given concentration for some heavy metals.
- **Biodegradation**: it biodegrades by at least 90% (by weight) within six months under controlled composting conditions (temperature of 58 +/- 2°C).
- **Disintegration**: it fragments into pieces smaller than 2 mm under controlled composting conditions within 12 weeks.
- **Eco-toxicity**: the compost obtained at the end of the process does not cause any negative effects.

A key limitation of these standards is the time taken for the materials to break-down (i.e. <2 mm within 12 weeks and 90% by weight after six months). Most industrial composting processes operate residence times of approximately eight weeks due to the cost of land and throughput required to make their operations profitable. As such, suitable processes that can compost end-of-life bio-based polymers to these standards are not typically commercially viable.

With respect to markets for recycled plastics, the critical issue here is the potential for mixing of biodegradable and non-biodegradable plastics. Where biodegradable non-drop-in polymers exhibit the same physical and aesthetic properties as fossil-based plastics, they can be unintentionally mixed (e.g. PLA and PET). This confusion can lead to biodegradable plastics contaminating other polymer streams due to incorrect classification at the point of disposal. Similarly, this misclassification can take place in reverse and lead to mainstream plastics being disposed of in composting facilities.

Technical barrier: Some biodegradable plastics exhibit the same characteristics as non-biodegradable materials (e.g. PLA and PET). This can lead to misclassification when materials are discarded, contaminating both recyclate streams and biological treatment facilities alike.

2.2.4.3. Global bio-plastics production by type

Despite the drawbacks described above and the very small market share of bio-plastics (1%) (European Bioplastics, 2016[20]), the market is slowly growing. Estimates of current production vary between 2 Mtpa (Institute for Bioplastics and Biocomposites, 2017[21]) and 4 Mpta (European Bioplastics, 2016[20]). Figure 2.4 shows the estimated current production of bio-plastics by polymer type. Current and predicted estimates for 2020 by polymer type and region are provided in Annex C.

Recent growth in bio-plastics has been driven by increases in production of drop-in polymers such as bio-based PE and PET. Overall, non-biodegradable plastics make up over 75% of bio-plastics production. Published market studies suggest that drop-in PET polymers will dominate growth in the bioplastics market over the next few years. Biodegradable bio-plastics are not expected to increase their share of the bio-plastics market.

Figure 2.4. **Global bio-plastics production by polymer type in 2016**

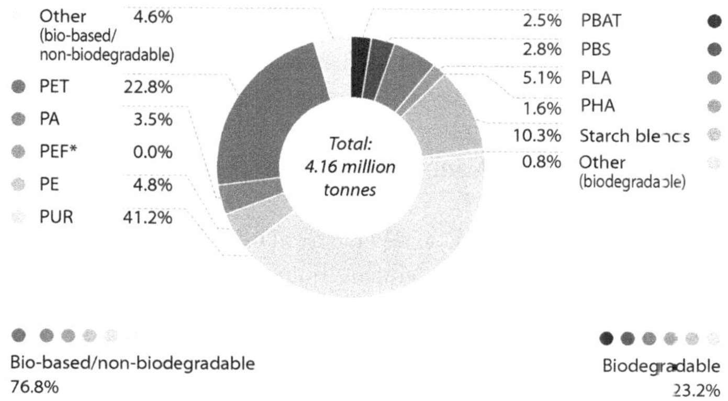

Source: European Bioplastics (2016[18]), *Bioplastic market data 2016,* http://bit.ly/2ySHyz7.

Notes

1. Data from the IEA and RRS indicates that hydrocarbon inputs represent upwards of 60% of the cost structure of virgin plastics production (The Economist, 2014[114]; CLP, 2017[115]).
2. CISION estimates production at ~34 Mt in 2014 and Geyer (2017) estimates total polymer resin and fibre production at 367 Mt for the same year. Therefore thermosets = 9.3% global production of all plastics.
3. Degradability includes biodegradability, oxo-degradation and photo degradation.
4. There are also standards for compostability, which can be viewed as a subset of biodegradability.

References

British Plastics Federation (2016), "The UK Plastics Industry: A Strategic Vision for Growth", http://bit.ly/2yfutkx (accessed on 26 March 2018). [89]

CISION (2015), *Global Thermosetting Plastics Market – Segmented by Type, Industry and Geography – Trends and Forecasts,* https://www.prnewswire.com/news-releases/global-thermosetting-plastics-market---segmented-by-type-industry-and-geography---trends-and-forecasts-2015-2020---reportlinker-review-300145372.html (accessed on 26 March 2018). [11]

COWI (2013), "Hazardous substances in plastics materials", www.miljodirektoratet.no/old/klif/publikasjoner/3017/ta3017.pdf (accessed on 26 March 2018). [13]

Crow (2016), *Top 10 Plastic Manufacturers,* http://polymerdatabase.com/Polymer%20Brands/Plastic%20Manufacturers.html (accessed on 26 March 2018). [10]

DiGangi, J. and J. Strakova (2015), "Toxic Toy or Toxic Waste: Recycling Pops into New Products", *IPEN,* http://ipen.org/sites/default/files/documents/toxic_toy_or_toxic_waste_2015_10-en.pdf (accessed on 26 March 2018). [16]

European Bioplastics (2016), "Bioplastics – Industry standards and labels", http://docs.european-bioplastics.org/2016/publications/fs/EUBP_fs_standards.pdf (accessed on 26 March 2018). [18]

European Bioplastics (2016), "Bioplastics market data", http://docs.european-bioplastics.org/publications/EUBP_Bioplastics_market_data_report_2016.pdf (accessed on 26 March 2018). [20]

Galloway, T. (2015), "Micro-and Nano-plastics and Human Health", http://dx.doi.org/10.1007/978-3-319-16510-3_13. [12]

Moss, E., A. Eidson and J. Jambeck (2017), "Sea of Opportunity: Supply Chain Investment Opportunities to Address Marine Plastic Pollution", http://plasticreport.vulcan.com/wp-content/uploads/2017/02/Sea-of-Opportunity_Summary_Final-Digital.pdf (accessed on 26 March 2018). [90]

Pivnenko, K. et al. (2016), "Recycling of plastic waste: Presence of phthalates in plastics from households and industry", *Waste Management*, Vol. 54, pp. 44-52, http://dx.doi.org/10.1016/j.wasman.2016.05.014. [15]

Plastics Europe (2016), "Plastics – the Facts 2017: An analysis of European plastics production, demand and waste data", https://www.plasticseurope.org/application/files/5715/1717/4180/Plastics_the_facts_2017_FINAL_for_website_one_page.pdf (accessed on 26 March 2018). [17]

Villanueva, A. and P. Eder (2014), "End-of-waste criteria for waste plastic for conversion", *European Commission: JRC Technical Reports*, http://publications.jrc.ec.europa.eu/repository/bitstream/111111111/33010/1/2014-jrc91637%20.pdf (accessed on 26 March 2018). [14]

Chapter 3

Recycling plastics

This chapter sets out the environmental benefits of plastics recycling and summarises current patterns of plastics waste generation and recycling. Lower greenhouse gas emissions and reduced leakage of plastics into the natural environment are highlighted as the two key environmental benefits of increased plastics waste collection and recycling. Plastics waste generation and recycling rates are discussed in the context of different regions, product categories, polymers, and waste streams, and data is presented for each. Finally, the chapter concludes with an assessment of the key drivers of plastics recycling, and how these might drive higher recycling rates in the future.

3.1. The environmental case for recycling plastics

3.1.1. Life cycle assessment

The environmental benefits and burdens of recycling relative to landfill and thermal treatment can be quantified using lifecycle assessment (LCA), an approach which takes into account the impacts of plastics at all stages of a product's lifecycle. For information, the key components ("system boundary") of a typical LCA for a plastic product are shown in Annex E.

LCA studies are complex and require a large amount of information to be gathered and synthesised to achieve a credible answer. There are many types of plastic, derived from different starting materials (Box 3.1), all of which have different impacts on the environment (see Tables D.1 and Table D.3 for detailed polymer specific LCA data). In addition, the production, consumption, and disposal of plastics have a variety of environmental impacts, not all of which are covered by LCA (for example, the impacts of marine plastics on wildlife through ingestion and entanglement). The uncertainty associated with these studies is high, and this is compounded by variations in system boundaries between different models.

Box 3.1. **Starting material**

The term "starting material" refers to a material which is ready to be formed into a shape or used as an additive. They differ from "raw materials" which require processing or transformation. The raw material for plastics is usually crude oil, however a plastic starting material would describe a polymer which has been extruded into a pellet, or in the case of a recycled material, a comminuted fragment or "flake".

One way to reduce uncertainty is to carry out meta-analysis of multiple studies to look for correlation between them. The UK's Waste and Resources Action Programme (Michaud, Farrant and Jan, 2010[19]) analysed 42 LCA studies to determine the most environmentally beneficial method of management for a range of commonly recycled materials, including plastics. The studies compared the environmental impact of seven thermoplastics across eight main impact categories: climate change potential, energy demand, water consumption, depletion of abiotic resources, acidification, photochemical oxidation, eutrophication and human toxicity. The report found that the environmental footprint of plastics recycling was small relative to that for thermal treatment or landfill (with landfill being the least favourable option). A summary of the findings relating to climate change potential is shown in Figure 3.1.

The majority of the climate change potential associated with the plastics lifecycle results from the production of virgin polymer. Large amounts of energy are required to refine the oil, crack the distilled constituents into monomers, and then synthesise the base starting materials. This process is highly energy-intensive, and was estimated to account for 400 million tonnes of greenhouse gas emissions (around 1% of the global total) in 2012 (EC, 2017[22]). The fossil fuel feedstock used in plastics production accounts for an additional 4% of global oil and gas production (Hopewell, Dvorak and Kosior, 2009[23]). Recycling of plastics avoids the use of much of this energy (Francis, Stadler and Roberts, 2016[24]), although considerable effort is also required to collect, sort and process the materials before they can re-enter the value chain as a starting material. Table 3.1 compares some of the impacts of production and transport between recycled and virgin plastics.

Figure 3.1. **Relative difference between the climate change impacts of different end-of-life options vs. recycling for plastics**

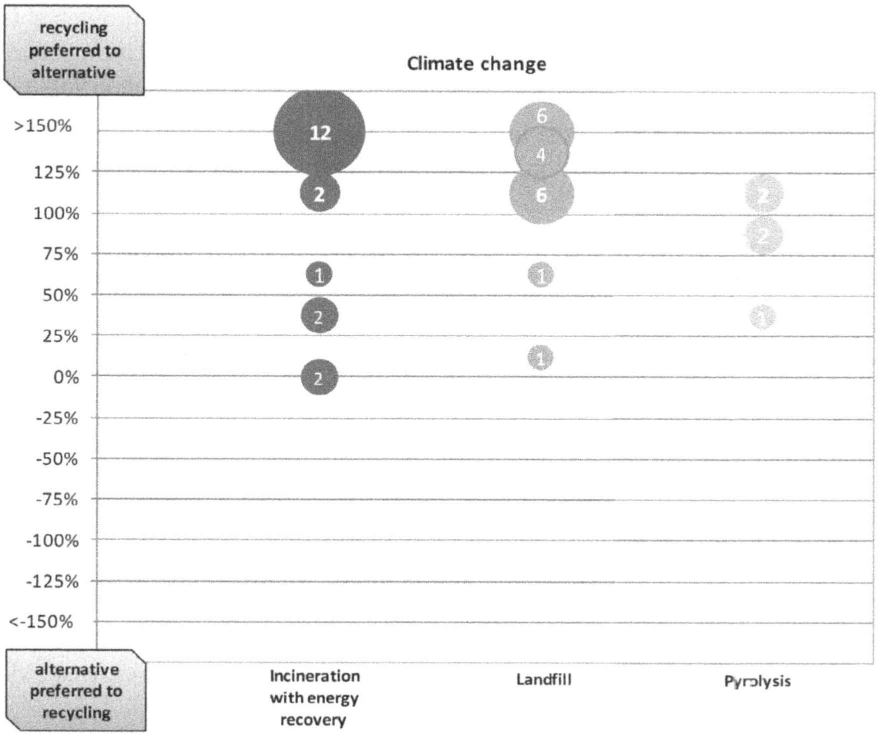

Note: The size of the "bubble" is proportional to the number of cases that have a value within a similar range.

Source: Michaud, Farrant and Jan (2010[19]), "Environmental benefits of recycling", *WRAP*, www.wrap.org.uk/sites/files/wrap/Environmental_benefits_of_recycling_2010_update.3b174d59.8816.pdf

Table 3.1. **Impact of production and transport activities on plastics recycling**

Activities	Virgin plastics	Recycled plastics
Energy consumption due to production	84 MJ/kg	7.97 MJ/kg
Energy consumption due to local transportation (recycling)	None	0.85 MJ/kg
Energy consumption due to export transportation (recycling)	None	1.53 MJ/kg
Atmospheric emission (CO_2) due to production	6 kg/kg	3.5 kg/kg
Atmospheric emission (CO_2) due to local transportation (recycling)	None	0.10 kg/kg
Atmospheric emission (CO_2) due to export transportation (recycling)	None	0.13 kg/kg

Source: Wong (2009[24]), *A study of plastic recycling supply chain*, http://bit.ly/2v:HK7L.

3.1.2. Ecosystem services and natural capital

Although LCA studies look in detail at a range of environmental impacts, they are not usually designed to quantify those impacts in terms of the economy. The concept of "natural capital" recognises that economic activity is supported by the natural environment (Defra, 2011[25]). This can be directly, through the provision of raw materials used for the production of goods and services, or indirectly, through the services provided by ecosystems (e.g. water purification, carbon sequestration, nutrient cycling, and mitigation of flood risk). A strong global economy therefore relies on natural resources to secure growth, both in the present and for future generations.

Natural capital refers to the stock of resources (renewable and non-renewable) which provide benefits that contribute to making human life possible and worth living. The benefits provided by nature can be broadly dived into three groups (The Nature Conservancy, 2016[26]):

- **Regulating services** are the ecosystem processes that regulate our environment such as prevention of erosion, coastal protection, biodiversity, water purification and carbon storage.
- **Provisioning services** provide tangible, harvestable, or extractable goods such as forests, mangroves, minerals, fish, shellfish and seaweed for food, algae, and health products.
- **Cultural services** are non-material benefits derived from nature such as beauty and recreation, as well as spiritual, intellectual and cultural benefits.

The proliferation of marine plastics, in the form of micro- or macro-plastics, has impacts on the quality of marine and coastal environments. Marine wildlife is harmed through ingestion of macro-plastics or entanglement, with negative implications for ecosystem health and the overall sustainability of fisheries.[1] Coastal tourism is also affected as tourists seek to avoid beaches known to have high concentrations of plastics litter. Taken together, the economic cost of these impacts has been estimated at USD 13 billion per year (UNEP, 2014[27]). Marine plastic debris has also been estimated to account for annual losses of USD 622 million for the tourism sector in the Asia Pacific Economic Area (McIlgorm, Campbell and Rule, 2011[28]).

Figure 3.2. **Estimated natural capital cost of plastics production and disposal by sector of origin**

USD million

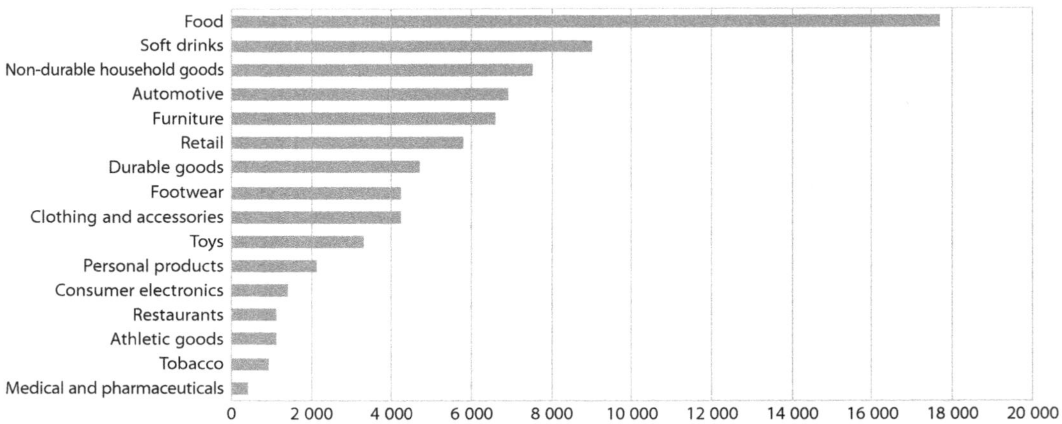

Note: The "estimated natural capital cost" shown in this graph represents the sum of the environmental damages resulting from plastics production and end-of-life management (but not those associated with plastics transport or use). Damages resulting from greenhouse gas emissions, plastics and chemical pollutants, and the consumption of water resources are included. Both the market costs (the impact of marine plastics litter on fisheries for example) and non-market costs (the disamenity generated by plastics pollution for coastal recreationalists) are aggregated together.

Source: UNEP (2014[25]), *Valuing Plastics: The Business Case for Measuring, Monitoring and Disclosing Plastics Use in the Consumer Goods Industry,* http://bit.ly/2vpC6Dx.

Plastic pollution also has impacts on soil and air quality. Fields and beaches are increasingly littered with packaging. Plastics break down very slowly in the soil (an important natural capital asset) due to absence of light and oxygen. Emissions to air are also important. Tyre wear and brake dust (containing plastics) contribute to a large portion of the particulate matter emissions from transport, and uncontrolled incineration of waste plastics threatens human and animal health.

An emerging concept in the field of ecosystem services is the concept of natural capital accounting. "Natural capital valuation" attributes monetary value to physical environmental impacts such as uncontrolled disposal of wastes, effectively putting a price on pollution. This is an important factor to consider when developing a case for plastics recycling at a global level as it allows companies and governments to put a price on their environmental impacts and prioritise the most important. A recent study by UNEP indicated that the natural capital costs of plastics waste in the consumer goods sector is USD 75 billion per year (UNEP, 2014[27]) (see Figure 3.2).

3.2. Plastics waste generation

3.2.1. Plastics waste generation data

The Global Waste Management Outlook estimates that 7 to 10 billion tonnes of waste is generated each year (ISWA, 2015[29]). Plastics waste generation is estimated at 302 Mtpa (Geyer, Jambeck and Law, 2017[1]), which represents around 3% to 4% of that total. Globally, plastics waste generation has been increasing as a consequence of several factors (Ocean Conservancy, 2015[30]):

- Municipal solid waste quantities are increasing as a result of population growth and urbanisation. Urban populations are reported to generate roughly 40% more waste than rural populations in low and middle-income countries.
- The proportion of plastics in the waste streams of emerging economies is increasing.
- Trends in the consumer packaging industry. Increasingly small products require more weight of packaging per kilogram of product. Similarly, improvements in food safety and enhanced preservation of freshness require additional packaging.
- An increasing variety of different packaging formats used to market products.

Global waste generation is expected to continue to increase during coming decades, driven in particular by waste growth in Africa (Hoornweg, Bhada-Tata and Kennedy, 2015[31]). The most recent and detailed study of global waste plastics generation and recycling was conducted by Geyer, Jambeck and Law (2017[1]). This study used global plastics production data combined with factors for waste generation and the average lifetime of products in different sectors, to derive estimates of total quantities of plastics waste generated and recycled. The underlying source data is relatively robust for Europe and the United States but of relatively poor quality for other regions so these estimates can only be considered indicative. However, it does serve to indicate the proportional growth in waste and in the quantities of plastics waste generally.

3.2.2. Plastics waste generation by polymer

The most common polymers in the waste stream are polyethylene (HDPE and LDPE) and polypropylene (PP), which account for just under half of all of the waste plastics produced (Figure 3.3). This is due to their widespread use in packaging plastics and single-use items, which are often discarded soon after they are purchased.

Figure 3.3. **Global plastics waste generation by polymer (million tonnes), 1950 to 2015**

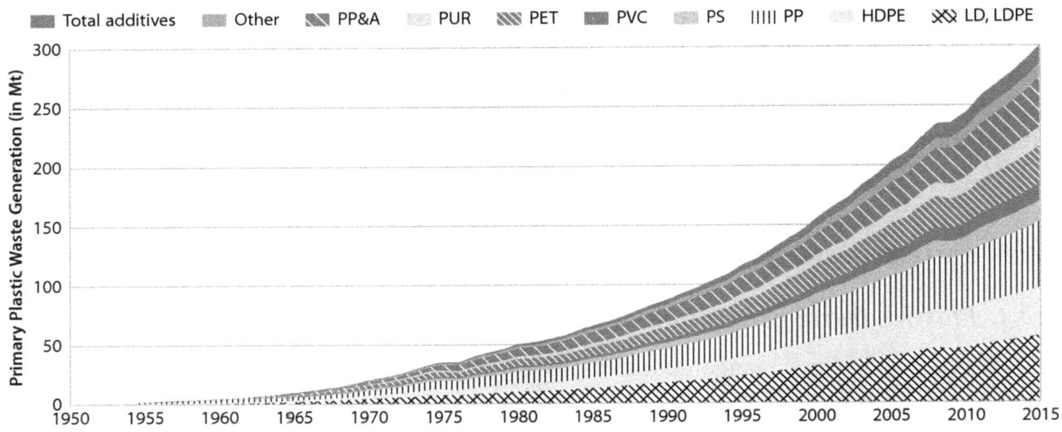

Source: Geyer et al. (2017), *Production, use, and fate of all plastics ever made*, http://bit.ly/2uBs8AT.

However, many plastics have a much longer lifetime. Items which have not become waste are sometimes described as being in the "use phase" or "stock". The difference in length of the use phase for different plastic products has implications for the different types of polymer that appear in the plastics waste stream. A good example of this is shown for PET in Figure 3.4. PET is used almost exclusively for single use packaging, therefore the difference between the amount generated and the amount that enters the use-phase is very small. Conversely, less than half of the PVC (a common construction material) produced each year becomes waste as it makes up the fabric of buildings (e.g. window frames) which have a long lifetime.

Figure 3.4. **Comparison of polymer production with the amount that becomes waste**

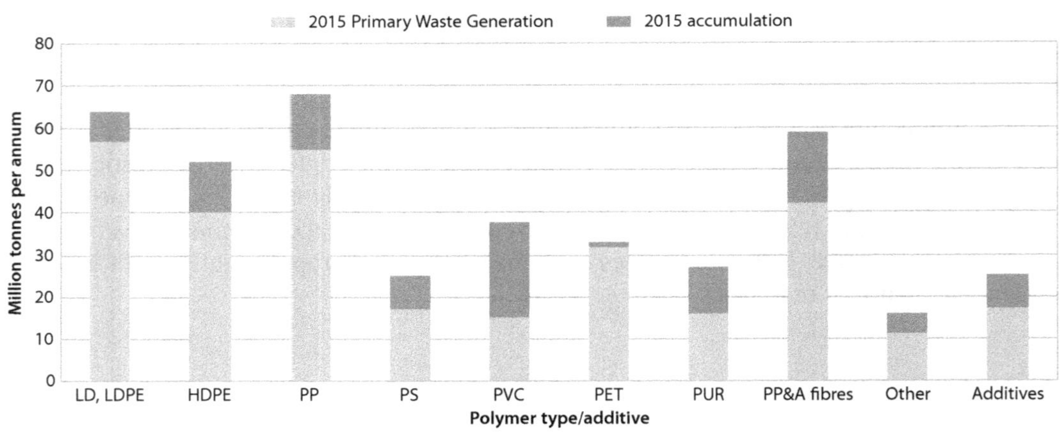

Source: Geyer et al. (2017), *Production, use, and fate of all plastics ever made*, http://bit.ly/2uBs8AT.

The example of construction is important because plastics are increasingly being used as an alternative to other building materials due to their versatility, low cost, and resistance to degradation in certain circumstances. This means that the stock of some plastics is increasing considerably year-on-year; totalling approximately 2 000 Mt since 1950 (Geyer, Jambeck and Law, 2017[11]).

Plastics waste generation can be broadly divided into post-industrial and post-consumer wastes. Both are briefly described below.

3.2.3. Post-consumer plastics waste

Post-consumer plastics waste includes all materials which have been sold or used following their manufacture. They can arise from domestic activities, such as food packaging, or other consumable goods, as well as commercial sources and through agriculture and construction. Increasingly, plastics are used in the manufacture of electrical equipment which is a becoming a major part of the global waste stream. Figure 3.5 shows the distribution of plastics waste generation across eight important product categories.

Figure 3.5. **Global plastics waste generation (million tonnes) by product category in 2015**

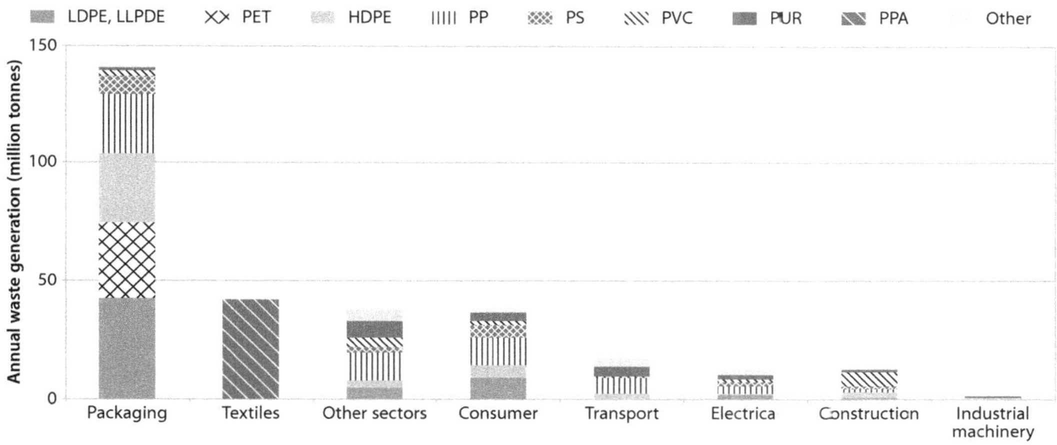

Note: The polymer breakdown for each product category has been translated on a proportional basis from 2015 production data.

Source: OECD, based on data from Geyer et al. (2017), *Production, use, and fate of all plastics ever made*, http://bit.ly/2uBs8AT.

Post-consumer plastics are difficult to collect due to their geographically dispersed generation and the wide range of different polymers in use. Commonly used packaging materials such as PET and HDPE are commonly captured for recycling due to their wide-spread use which improves the economy of scale for collectors. However, less-commonly used polymers do not offer the same economy of scale that makes their collection viable. Furthermore, where different polymers are combined within items (e.g. laminated packaging) or where plastics are combined with other materials (e.g. within electronic equipment), it is difficult and costly to separate them for recycling. Developments in packaging and product design (for example the use of complex combinations of polymers and other materials to assist with brand definition) have the potential to exacerbate this problem.

Economic barrier: Post-consumer plastics are costly to collect due to their geographical distribution and because of the wide range of polymers used, limiting economies of scale for less-common polymers. The combination of polymers of different types and with other materials within products also makes their separation for recycling difficult and costly.

Most higher-income countries have statutory waste collection regulations that require the collection of recyclate from households. This means that common packaging items are more likely to reach a re-processor. Middle and low-income countries may not have the same regimes, but informal or small scale commercial collectors often fill the gap if there is a sufficient market for these materials.

Post-consumer plastics often also contain impurities such as food residues, non-target materials, and non-recyclable materials. This degree of contamination depends significantly on the behaviour of waste producers, and can therefore be influenced through education campaigns provided through signage, instructional literature, and other communications (e.g. TV and radio information). The provision of suitable facilities also plays an important part in encouraging people to separate materials in such a way that they can be easily recycled. For example, providing a street bin with a restricted aperture to prevent contrary items from being deposited will encourage the correct materials to be deposited.

Economic barrier: Post-consumer plastics are commonly contaminated with non-recyclable and non-target materials. This leads to materials being rejected for recycling and increases the processing costs to remove contamination.

Another example of post-consumer waste can be found in the construction sector. At the end of their life, buildings can be crudely demolished, resulting in a mixture of materials which can be landfilled as is, or potentially processed in a specialist facility to attempt recovery of valuable materials. At present, most plastics are not recovered from demolished buildings; the low material value and difficulty of extracting or disassembling them from the demolition matrix makes recovery uneconomic. This may change in the future if "selective dismantlement" or "deconstruction" of building components becomes more commonplace. These activities involve either the extraction of materials prior to demolition, or an entire system of work where a building is disassembled into its constituent materials.

Another growing but currently under-exploited source for plastics is from the interior of end-of-life vehicles. Approximately 20% of their content is composed of mixed plastics (Recycling and Waste World, 2015[32]), a figure that is likely to increase as car manufacturers follow the trend away from metal vehicle components towards plastics.

3.2.4. Post-industrial plastics waste

Post-industrial (sometimes referred to as pre-consumer) waste plastics are easier to collect as there are fewer points of generation. They also tend to be composed of a single type of polymer and are less likely to contain impurities.

Impurities that arise as a result of their manufacturing are also likely to be more predictable than from post-consumer sources as manufacturing tends to follow a repeatable process. As such, post-industrial waste plastics are more commonly recycled than post-consumer wastes, provided that they arise in sufficient quantity. If they are not recycled in-house by the manufacturer, they are also more likely to receive a higher price when sold to a third party re-processor because relatively little effort will be needed to remove contamination.

Detailed global data are not readily available on post-industrial plastics waste, but levels of post-industrial waste generation are thought to be considerably lower than for post-consumer waste. For example, it is estimated that post-industrial plastics waste generation is around 0.25-0.3 Mtpa in the United Kingdom. This compares to an estimated 3.9 Mtpa of post-consumer plastics waste. Conversely, recycling rates for post-industrial wastes are much higher. For example, in the UK approximately 90% of post-industrial plastics waste is thought to be recycled (ISWA, 2014[33]) compared to approximately 22% of post-consumer waste.

3.2.5. Additives

Overall, additives are estimated to comprise 7% all plastics production by mass (Geyer, Jambeck and Law, 2017[1]). Table 3.2 summarises the main types of additives, their relative proportions of production and the estimated quantities that become part of the waste stream.

Table 3.2. **Proportion of additives by type used in global plastics resin (non-fibre) waste**

Additive type	Proportion of additive used in global plastics production	Mass of additives that became waste in 2015 (Mt)
Plasticisers	34%	7.2
Fillers	28%	5.9
Flame retardants	13%	2.7
Antioxidants	6%	1.3
Heat stabilisers	5%	1.1
Impact modifiers	5%	1.1
Other	4%	0.8
Colourants	2%	0.4
Lubricants	2%	0.4
Light stabilisers	1%	0.2
Totals	**100%**	**21.1**

Note: Proportions are based on estimated additive use between 2000 and 2014 and applied to estimated waste plastic generated in 2105.

Source: Geyer, Jambeck and Law (2017[1]), *Production, use, and fate of all plastics ever made*, http://bit.ly/2uBs8AT.

3.3. Plastics recycling performance

3.3.1. Global plastics recycling performance

Recycling of post-industrial plastics is well-established and has been relatively stable over recent decades. In contrast, recycling of post-consumer plastics is less common, but has increased steadily since the 1980s as municipal recycling schemes have developed in high income countries (see Figure 3.6). Incineration has followed a similar trend with a steep increase over recent years as additional incineration capacity has been developed in Europe and North America.

At present, around 14%-18% of waste plastics generation is collected for recycling (EMF, 2016[34]; Geyer, Jambeck and Law, 2017[1]). Another 24% is thermally treated (e.g. by incineration, gasification or pyrolysis), while the remainder is disposed of in controlled, landfill, uncontrolled landfill, or the natural environment. The latter is thought to account for between 4 and 12 Mtpa of plastics waste each year.

Figure 3.6. **Global plastics waste generation, recycling, incineration, and disposal: 1950 to 2015**

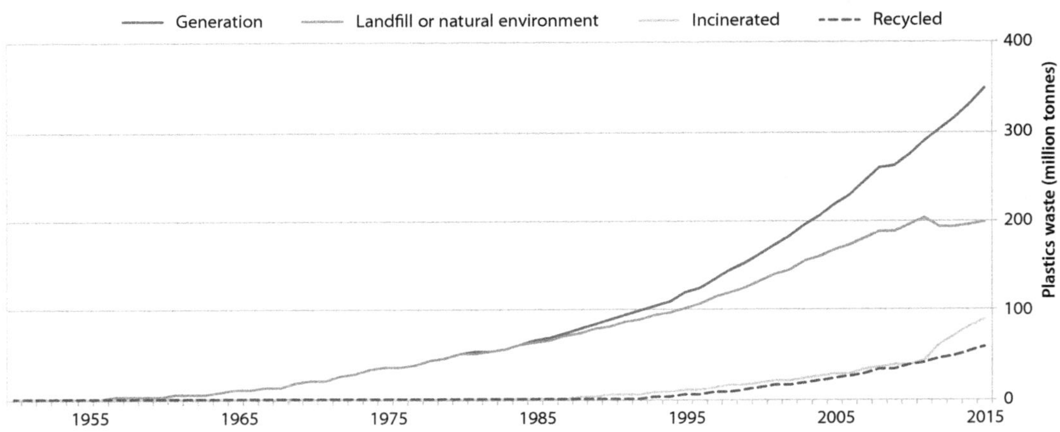

Source: OECD, based on data from Geyer, Jambeck and Law (2017[1]), *Production, use, and fate of all plastics ever made*, http://bit.ly/2uBs8AT.

3.3.2. Regional variations in plastics recycling performance

There are large differences in plastics recycling rates across regions and countries (Box 3.2), and across different polymers. Data for the European Union (Eurostat,(n.d.)[35]) and for the United States (provided by the United States Environmental Protection Agency (Recycling and Waste World, 2015[32])) are the most comprehensive. In addition, Plastics Europe provides relatively detailed data on plastics recycling, based on market research undertaken by the consultancy firm Consultic. The questionnaire responses provided by OECD members also provided some data for Australia and Japan. Data for other countries is not readily available.

Box 3.2. **Calculating recycling rates**

In Europe, recycling rates are typically calculated as the proportion of materials recycled as a percentage of total waste generated. However, the method for doing so is not standardised; there are two broad concepts for calculation:

- Weigh the material that leaves the sorting plant or enters the recycling plant
- Weigh the material that is successfully processed

Each method will yield different results because not all of the waste entering the system is recyclable. Non-recyclable residues can be a significant proportion of sorted materials in many cases. When the latter of the two methods is used, it is challenging to get accurate data for any material processed abroad, leading to an inflation of the amount of material recycled.

Box 3.2. **Calculating recycling rates** *(continued)*

Further uncertainty arises because the Waste Hierarchy is not applied consistently across nations. This means that terms such as energy recovery and material recycling may be used interchangeably or are applied to different processes. Other disparities result from the classification of waste from mining and agriculture which may be poorly regulated in some nations.

EU members have underlying specific targets for particular packaging materials such as metals, plastics, paper, wood and glass (see Annex H). In contrast to the above method, progress to these targets is based on the proportion of material actually recycled as a percentage of total material placed on the market (POM). One of the benefits of this method, which is also proposed for other materials, is that the success of an intervention to increase recycling isn't affected by the amount of material arising from an unconnected activity.

Figure 3.7 shows a combined set of data based on these sources.[2] It illustrates that plastics recycling rates in Europe have steadily increased, driven by statutory targets at the European Union level. Recycling rates in the United States have increased steadily but have not yet exceeded 10%. The single data point for Japan signals levels that are closer to those in the European Union. The single data points for Australia fall in between the US and European rates.

Figure 3.7. **Plastics recycling in the EU, USA, Australia and Japan (2005-15)**

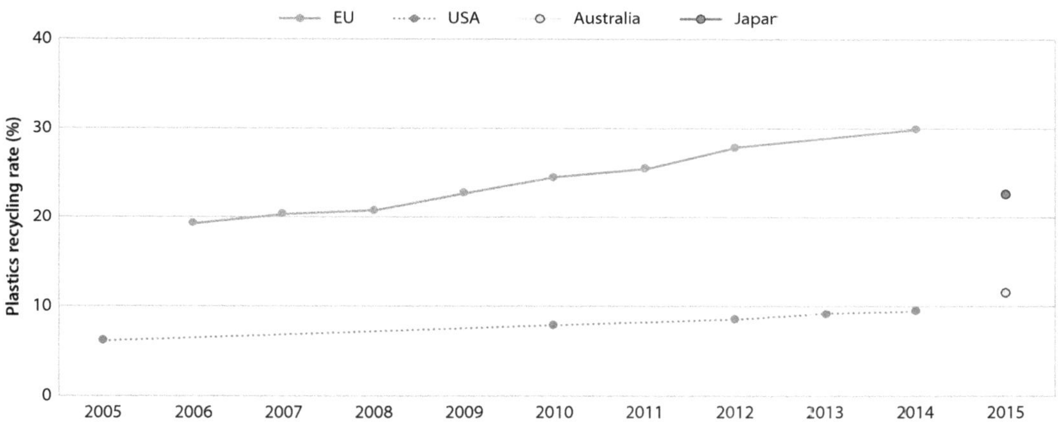

Source: Plastics Europe (2016[17]), *Plastics – the Facts 2017: An analysis of European plastics production, demand and waste data*, http://bit.ly/2C39H7H ; United States Environmental Protection Agency (2014[33]), *Advancing Sustainable Materials Management*, http://bit.ly/2wNu9ey ; OECD member questionnaires.

3.3.3. Recycling performance by sector

Comprehensive quantitative data on the levels of plastics recycling for different sectors is not readily available. However, data for Australia provides a good illustration of the relative levels of recycling for different sectors (Table 3.3).

Packaging plastics are the most commonly recycled type of plastics. As discussed in Section 2.1, packaging plastics represent the single largest market for plastics and the largest fraction of plastics waste generation due to their relatively short use-cycle. Packaging plastics are easy to identify, relatively easy to separate from materials in the waste stream and, depending upon quality, have relatively high values in the market for recycled plastics As such, recycling of packaging plastics has driven overall plastics recycling. In many countries, particularly those in the EU, this increase in the proportion of packaging plastics recycling has been driven by producer responsibility legislation and accompanying targets (see Figure 3.8). As illustrated in Table 3.4, the recycling of packaging plastics is significantly higher than waste plastics from other sectors where there is considerable scope for increasing recycling rates.

Table 3.3. **Australian plastics consumption by waste stream (2015/16)**

Application area	Recovery (tonnes)	Consumption(tonnes)	Recycling rate
Packaging	263 000	844 300	31.1%
Electrical & electronic	8 200	149 200	5.5%
Agriculture	4 500	84 100	5.3%
Automotive	4 400	175 200	2.5%
Built environment	8 700	563 800	1.6%
Other application areas	14 100	598 700	2.4%
Unidentified applications	26 000	496 700	5.2%
Total	**328 900**	**2 912 000**	**11.3%**

Source: OECD questionnaire responses.

Figure 3.8. **Comparison of recycling rates in the EU for all plastics and for packaging plastics (2005-15)**

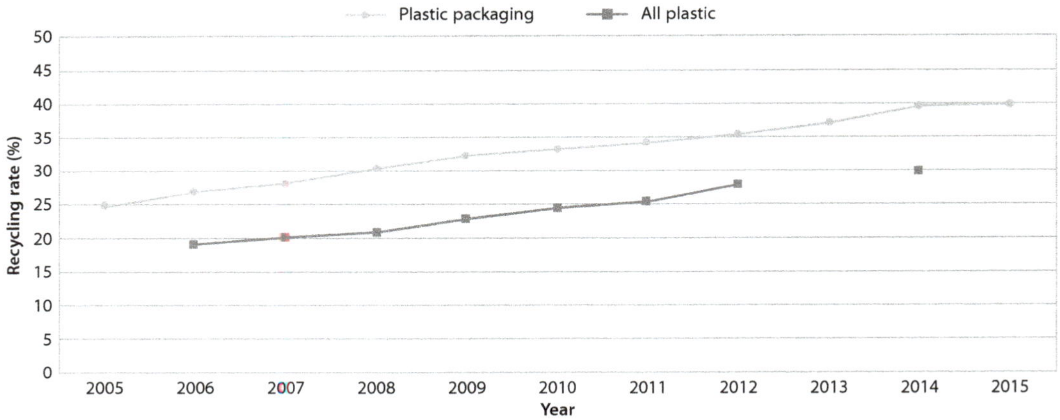

Table 3.4. **Summary of recycling rates for key polymers**

Polymer	USA*	Japan***
PET	19.1%	85%
HDPE	10.5%	16%****
LDPE	5.8%	
PS	1.3%	21%
PP	0.8%	15%
EPS	No data	No data
PVC	0.0%	24%

Note: *2014, **2016, ***2015, ****Combined data for HDPE and LDPE.

Source: OECD questionnaire responses.

3.3.4. Recycling performance by polymer

Table 3.4 shows the most recent reported data for key polymers for Japan and the United States (see Annex J for further information obtained from the OECD questionnaires). These data should be treated with caution, as the definitions used are not clear. However, they do serve to illustrate that PET, HDPE and LDPE are the most widely recycled types of polymer. This is primarily the effect of the high proportion of these materials' use in packaging. PET is the most commonly recycled polymer. Recycled PET has a relatively high value on international markets, driven significantly by demand in China over the last decade.

As Figure 2.2 shows, PP is also produced and consumed in large quantities and forms a key packaging material. However, it is technically more challenging to separate from similar polymers, making it more difficult to recycle. As the data in Table 3.4 illustrates, PP is not recycled at the same level as PET, HDPE and LDPE.

Annex J provides a summary of other data provided by OECD Questionnaire responses on polymer-specific recycling performance. Similar polymer-specific data for other countries was not available at the time of writing. This would be particularly useful to obtain because it would provide clarity on the relative level of circularity within the plastics market and enable targeted interventions based on polymer type.

Economic barrier: Data on the generation and fate of waste plastics is limited and of poor quality, particularly outside Europe and the United States. This limits the ability of actors in the market to make evidence-based, strategic decisions and interventions.

3.4. Future plastics waste generation and recycling

Predicting future generation and recycling rates for waste plastics is challenging given the diversity of polymers and applications, and the wide range of contexts and accompanying legislative regimes that apply. Between 1994 and 2014, plastics recycling rates increased globally by 0.7% annually. If this continues at the same rate, then the global recycling rate for plastics will be 44% by 2050 (see Figure 3.9). By the same logic, the global incineration rate of waste plastics will be 50% by 2050, leaving 6% per annum being disposed of in landfill or water. However, by this time, roughly 12 000 Mt will already have been disposed of into the natural environment (UNEP, 2014[27]).

A wide range of factors are involved in driving up plastics recycling, some of which are summarised below:

- **Statutory targets for recycling**. Statutory targets for recycling have been a key driver for increasing recycling, particularly in Europe. Continued legislative intervention is likely to be required to help continue to increase recycling of plastics. For example, the EU's circular economy package which is due to be voted upon by the European Parliament, includes challenging targets for plastics recycling.
- **Private sector activity, primarily driven by consumer pressure**. Major plastics manufacturers and consumer brands are increasingly recognising that poorly managed plastics not only have a significant impact on the environment but also represent a significant brand and reputational risk. A number of private sector operators are taking action to increase the recycling or substitution of plastics, particularly packaging plastics.

- **Technology innovation**. A wide range of innovation initiatives are underway to address technical barriers to post-consumer recycling (e.g. the Ellen MacArthur Global Plastics Protocol (EMF, 2017[36]). For example, there are a number of initiatives seeking to find ways that will allow black PP packaging to be identified by automatic sorting units (WRAP, 2015[37]). A break-through of this sort could have a significant effect on the recyclability of PP, a key element of packaging that is not typically recycled. Similar challenges also exist for other sectors and types of plastics (for example, for the use of black thermosets in consumer electronics); innovations of this type could have widespread benefits.

Figure 3.9. **Projected increase in plastics waste generation and recovery by 2050**

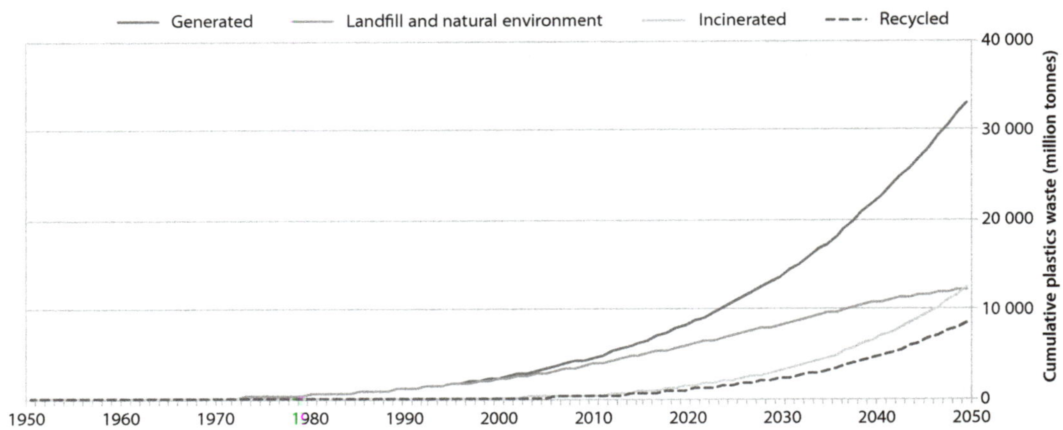

Note: Data for 2015 to 2050 are based on projections that assume (i) a slowing growth in waste plastics generation, from 5% per year in 2015 to 3% per year in 2050, and (ii) an annual increase in recycling rates of 0.7% per year.

Source: OECD, based on data from Geyer, Jambeck and Law (2017[1]), *Production, use, and fate of all plastics ever made*, http://bit.ly/2uBs8AT.

It is widely accepted that, where it is economically feasible, recycling plastics is environmentally preferable to Energy from Waste (EfW) treatment (see Section 3.1). That said, EfW has the potential to provide an outlet for waste plastics that cannot currently be recycled, and which would otherwise be disposed to landfill. It could also provide a suitable outlet for bio-based plastics, given their biogenic origin. Experience in Europe, where EfW is relatively well-developed, suggests that EfW treatment is not necessarily a barrier to high recycling rates (e.g. Germany has both Energy from Waste capacity and a high recycling rate).

However, as a treatment option for waste plastics, EfW could potentially compete with recycling as an outlet for waste plastics. Waste plastics have a high calorific value and low moisture content, making them a desirable feedstock compared to other types of waste (e.g. organics which have a relatively low calorific value). The capital intensive nature of EfW facilities also means that municipal authorities often contract over a long period (e.g. 25 years) and are committed to provide a minimum quantity of waste to an EfW operator. This could potentially prevent the growth of plastics recycling over a long period (so-called "lock-in").

Environmental barrier: There is a risk that, in specific contexts, EfW will compete for access to waste plastics as a feedstock thus locking the management of plastics into a less-preferred option in environmental terms.

Notes

1. Ingestion of plastics, or entanglement in them, has been documented in around 500 species of marine mammals, fish, and seabirds, with clear negative consequences for marine ecosystems and the fishing industry (UNEP, 2016[113]).

2. These data should be treated with caution as the underlying data has not been validated. The data point for Japan in particular may not represent comparable data due to the way in which Japan collects and reports plastics recycling data. The most comprehensive data on plastics recycling is available for Europe. This is presented in Annex I.

References

Defra (2011), "The Economics of Waste and Waste Policy", https://www.gov.uk/government/uploads/system/uploads/attachment_data/file/69500/pb13548-economic-principles-wr110613.pdf (accessed on 26 March 2018). [25]

EMF (2017), *Industry endorses plan to recycle 70% of plastics globally*, https://www.ellenmacarthurfoundation.org/news/new-plastics-economy-report-2-launch (accessed on 26 March 2018). [36]

EMF (2016), "The New Plastics Economy", https://www.ellenmacarthurfoundation.org/assets/downloads/EllenMacArthurFoundation_TheNewPlasticsEconomy_15-3-16.pdf (accessed on 26 March 2018). [34]

EUROPEN (2009), "Modern Beverage Container Policy", www.embcpar.pt/folder/documento/81_2009%20Modern%20Beverage%20Container%20Policy.pdf (accessed on 26 March 2018). [41]

Eurostat((n.d.)), *Environmental Data Centre on Waste*, http://ec.europa.eu/eurostat/web/environment/waste (accessed on 27 March 2018). [35]

Francis, L., B. Stadler and C. Roberts (2016), *Materials processing : a unified approach to processing of metals, ceramics and polymers*, https://www.sciencedirect.com/science/book/9780123851321 (accessed on 26 March 2018). [24]

Geyer, R., J. Jambeck and K. Law (2017), "Production, use, and fate of all plastics ever made", *Science Advances*, Vol. 3/7, p. e1700782, http://dx.doi.org/10.1126/sciadv.1700782. [1]

Hoornweg, D., P. Bhada-Tata and C. Kennedy (2015), "Peak Waste: When Is It Likely to Occur?", *Journal of Industrial Ecology*, Vol. 19/1, pp. 117-128, http://dx.doi.org/10.1111/jiec.12165. [31]

Institute for Bioplastics and Biocomposites (2017), "Biopolymers", https://www.ifbb-hannover.de/files/IfBB/downloads/faltblaetter_broschueren/Biopolymers-Facts-Statistics_2017.pdf (accessed on 26 March 2018). [21]

ISWA (2015), *Global Waste Management Outlook*, www.iswa.org/nc/home/news/news-detail/article/press-release-global-waste-management-outlook-gwmo/109/ (accessed on 26 March 2018). [29]

Michaud, J., L. Farrant and O. Jan (2010), "Environmental benefits of recycling", *WRAP*, www.wrap.org.uk/sites/files/wrap/Environmental_benefits_of_recycling_2010_update.3b174d59.8816.pdf (accessed on 26 March 2018). [19]

Ocean Conservancy (2015), "Stemming the Tide: Land-based strategies for a plastic-free ocean", https://oceanconservancy.org/wp-content/uploads/2017/04/full-report-stemming-the.pdf (accessed on 26 March 2018). [30]

The Nature Conservancy (2016), *Ecosystem Services*, http://oceanwealth.org/ecosystem-services/ (accessed on 26 March 2018). [26]

UNEP (2014), "The Business Case for Measuring, Managing and Disclosing Plastic Use in the Consumer Goods Industry", https://wedocs.unep.org/bitstream/handle/20.500.11822/9238/-Valuing%20plastic%3A%20the%20business%20case%20for%20measuring%2C%20managing%20and%20disclosing%20plastic%20use%20in%20the%20consumer%20goods%20industry-2014Valuing%20plasticsF.pdf?sequence=8&isA (accessed on 26 March 2018). [27]

Wong, C. (2009), "A Study of Plastic Recycling Supply Chain", https://www.ciltuk.org.uk/portals/0/documents/pd/seedcornwong.pdf (accessed on 26 March 2018). [91]

WRAP (2015), *Recyclability of black plastic packaging*, www.wrap.org.uk/content/recyclability-black-plastic-packaging-0 (accessed on 26 March 2018). [37]

Chapter 4

The recycled plastics industry

This chapter presents an overview of the plastics recycling industry. It begins with an overview of the recycled plastics value chain, from initial waste collection and sorting activities through to the production of recycled plastics suitable for re-introduction into the economy. The second part of the chapter then looks at each stage of the value chain in more detail. The market structure associated with plastics waste collection, sorting, and reprocessing is described along with the key actors and technologies involved in each of these activities

4.1. Overview of the recycled plastics supply chain

The process by which waste plastics move from the place at which they are generated to the point at which they become a recycled material is complex. Heterogeneous and dispersed waste generation contributes to this complexity which, for plastics, is also compounded by the large range of polymers involved.

Many actors are involved, ranging from informal waste collectors that collect recyclables to earn income, to governmental organisations that typically have a statutory duty to manage waste on behalf of their citizens (OECD, 2013[38]). The private sector also plays a key role in waste management, providing services to businesses and citizens to treat and dispose of waste materials. In many countries, businesses operate via government funded contracts, but also often through independent entrepreneurship. Community-based organisations and non-governmental organisations are also commonly involved in plastics recycling in many contexts (GIZ, 2013[39]).

An overview of the structure of the recycled plastics industry is shown in Figure 4.1. In practice, individual processes may be carried out in isolation or combined at a single location. This is often the case with the collection and preparation of waste materials for sale, or with sorting, flaking, washing and palletisation processes. As discussed above, these activities can be carried out by the informal sector, by commercial operators, or by publicly owned organisations.

Figure 4.1. **Overview of the plastics industry structure**

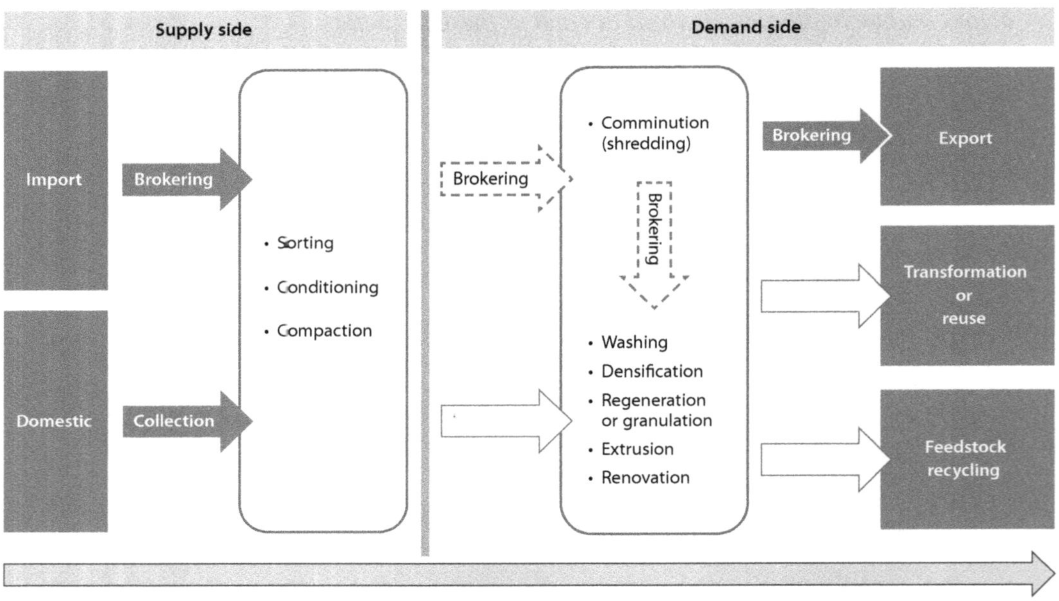

Note: The term broker refers to an entity that markets materials on behalf of another party for a cut of the revenue. Brokers may intervene at any stage of the value chain from collection and containment at the point of production, through to the marketing of flake or pelletised outputs from recyclers. In recent years in the UK and Europe, there has been an increase in the amount of business being carried out by outsourcing companies that broker waste management and facilities management services.

Source: Adapted from Villanueva and Eder (2014[14]), *End-of-waste criteria for waste plastic for conversion*, http://bit.ly/1y7ADLM.

Although trade in recycled plastics is global, the structure of the recycled plastics supply chain (and the waste management system of which it forms a part) varies significantly between countries, sub-national regions, and even cities. There are numerous operating models involving different combinations of: wholly municipal-operated services; wholly private sector delivered services; joint public and private services; publicly-owned municipal services. These can operate together with or alongside the activities of micro and small enterprises, community-based organisations, non-governmental organisations and the informal sector.

Detailed data on the structure of the industry is not readily available and there are no clear distinctions between operator models that are applied in different contexts. Furthermore, there is often confusion between converters who use recycled materials ("converters") and true recyclers that create the starting materials themselves.

However, there are general differences that can be observed between low and high-income country contexts (Table 4.1). Each of the three main parts of the recycled plastics supply chain are discussed in further detail in the sections below.

Table 4.1. **Key factors affecting the recycled plastics supply chain in low, middle and high-income country contexts**

Stage	Low income	Middle income	High income
Collection	• Informal sector plays a key role. • Mechanisation of collection limited to wealthy urban areas. • Recycling likely to be informal or SME-led. Few municipal-led plastics recycling schemes in this context.	• Some municipal-led recycling schemes, particularly in urban areas. • Some mechanisation of collection, particularly in urban areas. Informal sector often still plays a key role	• Municipal-led plastics recycling schemes common. • Collection systems highly mechanised.
Primary sorting	• Manual sorting is common. • Mechanical sorting normally limited to balers for compaction.	• Some mechanisation • Where informal sector is active, manual separation also likely to be common.	• Highly mechanised and capital intensive to maximise recovery of valuable plastics.
Recycling	• Waste plastics typically exported although there may be some simple recycling process used for plastics (e.g. manufacture of paving slabs from waste plastic bags) (WasteAid, 2017[40])	• Waste plastics typically exported for recycling but there may be some local recycling industry in some contexts.	• Waste plastics exported but some local capacity in some countries for high value plastics.

Economic barrier: There is limited information available on the structure of the industry. There is also confusion over terminology (e.g. variations over what constitutes a "recycler"). This lack of data restricts evidence-based strategic decisions and interventions.

4.2. Collection and containment methods

4.2.1. Municipal waste plastics collection

Waste plastics generated by households make up the majority of municipal waste plastics generation, and consist almost entirely of single use packaging. Three main systems exist for collecting these materials: kerbside collection, communal collection, and deposit return systems. The informal sector also plays a key role in waste collection in low and lower-middle income countries and is discussed separately below.

4.2.1.1. Kerbside waste collection

Waste collection systems vary considerably across countries, regions, and cities. Households in high income countries generally have access to kerbside collection. This is generally organised by local governments, who often have a statutory duty to segregate materials including plastics for separate collection from residual waste. Many models exist for the kerbside collection of dry recyclates. These can be broadly summarised as single stream (comingled), dual stream (two separate mixtures), and multi-stream (separate compartments on vehicle for each material).

Formal kerbside waste collection systems are less established in low and middle income countries. In the absence of services being provided by local authorities, private contractors may provide the only alternative. In these situations, waste may be stored on the premises of the house owner, dumped or burned in the street, or transported to informal dumpsites further away. These methods of uncontrolled disposal, lead to increases in disease vectors and environmental pollution. Waste collection rates in different global regions are thought to vary considerably (UNEP, 2016[4]):

- North America (100%)
- Latin America and Caribbean (80% to 100%)
- Africa (25% to 70%)
- Europe (80% to 100%)
- Asia (50% to 90%)

Overall, it is estimated that as many as two billion people do not have access to basic municipal waste collection services (UNEP, 2016[4]). It is likely that substantial quantities of waste plastics are not collected, and instead escape into the wider environment. If each of these individuals generate 0.25 kg of waste per person per day, and if 10% of the waste stream is plastics, then this leakage would amount to around 15 million tonnes of waste plastics per year.

Technical challenge: An estimated 2 billion people globally do not have access to basic waste collection services, meaning that large quantities of waste plastics are not collected at all.

4.2.1.2. Communal collection

The other main organised collection system for dry recyclate is via communal bins (or "bring banks"), which require residents to transport their waste to central collection hubs. These systems can be considered as an extension of household collection systems. They are relatively common in low and middle-income country contexts (as well as some high income countries) where their lower operational cost makes them an attractive option for municipalities.

Communal collection systems need to be supported by public engagement and associated regulatory enforcement to encourage householders to transfer their wastes to communal locations rather than burn or dump them close to their homes. With respect to plastics recycling, these systems can be associated with lower recycling rates as householders are required to carry materials separately to the location. In the UK for instance, the recycling of plastics increased considerably as authorities began to collect them from directly from households rather than from communal bins.

4.2.1.3. Deposit return

Deposit return schemes are operated for certain materials in various countries, including Austria, Germany, the Netherlands, and Switzerland. These schemes have declined over the last few decades, but there has been a recent renewed interest in this approach. For example, the Scottish Government recently announced plans to implement a deposit return scheme for containers. The benefit of deposit return schemes for plastics recycling is that the material is collected by the retailers and returned to the manufacturer via reverse logistics, representing a potentially significant efficiency improvement. Deposit return schemes also yield a very pure, uncontaminated stream of recyclate; post-consumer waste can achieve quality levels much closer to those associated with post-industrial waste.

So called "refill and deposit schemes" (Villanueva and Eder, 2014[14]) have seen a decline in recent years as it has been considered that they create a barrier to cross-border trade (EUROPEN, 2009[41]). An example provided by JRC (2014), describes a crate recycling system in Finland which was removed in 2008 as it created in international trade barrier. In another example, Denmark expanded the scope of its system to encompass non-refillable mineral water bottles (Pro Europe,(n.d.)[42]).

4.2.1.4. Informal sector

The informal sector plays a key role in the waste management system in low and middle-income countries. It is thought that there are over 20 million informal sector recyclers globally (IIED, 2016[43]) and that the indirect services they provide to municipalities in the form of waste collection and recycling are considerable.

The relatively high recycling rates achieved in low and lower-middle income countries (20-40%) can be largely attributed to the informal sector. Indeed, there is some evidence that higher income countries have slightly lower recycling rates due to informal sector workers being displaced by formal waste management systems (UNEP, 2014[27]).

Informal sector waste collectors depend upon the revenue from the sale of plastic items, and will typically only focus on high value plastics unless they are also paid separately for providing general waste collection services. Low value plastics will either be ignored or discarded. Anecdotally it is understood that, in this context, "dematerialisation" of plastics packaging (i.e. designing packaging that uses less material, for cost-saving and/or environmental reasons) can actually dis-incentivise informal collection. In countries where the informal sector plays a key role in collecting waste plastics, the development of formal waste management systems that do not integrate well with the existing informal sector can create a risk of lower recycling rates.

4.2.2. Bulking and transport

Waste plastics arise where people live and work, and require considerable consolidation and transport before they can be economically processed. In higher income countries, this typically begins at the point of collection, often via specially adapted vehicles which allow the separation of recyclates from other waste. In lower income countries, the collection methods include smaller trucks, motorbikes, and animal driven carts.

Plastics are comparatively light-weight, and in the case of packaging, contain trapped air which reduces the efficiency of collection vehicles. Baling is common following delivery of loose material to an intermediate local transfer station. This allows articulated bulk road vehicles to become a cost-effective method of transport.

In lower income contexts where facilities for compaction may not be available, or where the distance to re-processing facilities is high, plastics are often not collected at all as transport is not cost effective. Waste plastics may instead be stored or burned openly. In Europe, plastics were one of the last materials to be added to the materials collection portfolios of local authorities because of their low value and high transport costs. It is likely that they would not be collected in higher income countries if regulation was not in place to drive the process.

4.2.3. Commercial waste plastics collection

As with the plastics contained in municipal solid waste, commercial plastics primarily consist of packaging. However, it is mainly distribution film and EPS rather than food and beverage containers. Collection of these materials is likely to be more profitable because the material is often more consistent, free from contamination, and arises in larger quantities (Villanueva and Eder, 2014[14]).

4.2.4. Industrial waste plastics collection

Plastics waste arising from industrial processes is often generated by the plastics industry itself, with well-established supply routes. The flow charts in Figure 4.2 and Figure 4.3 illustrate the supply chain for post-consumer and post-industrial waste respectively, highlighting the differences between how the two categories of material are collected, contained, transported and treated.

4.2.5. Collection of waste thermoset plastics

Thermosets also arise in municipal solid waste streams but, unlike the single-use packaging items that are the main focus of municipal plastics recycling schemes, they form part of items which typically have a longer life (e.g. cars, sports equipment and domestic appliances). Thermoset plastics from municipal sources are often combined with other materials, making them difficult to separate for recycling. As such, they are seldom collected separately from municipal sources, unless as part of schemes focusing on specific items (e.g. waste electrical and electronic equipment or household appliances).

The majority of thermoset plastics that are collected for recycling are thought to be collected from industrial and commercial sources (e.g. from the automotive sector) or from companies processing municipal waste streams that contain some thermoset plastics (e.g. such as refrigerators).

> **Technical barrier:** Collection systems for thermosets are not well-established and are thought to be limited to commercial and industrial sources and some specific items that arise in the municipal waste (e.g. household appliances).

Figure 4.2. **Material flow for post-consumer plastics**

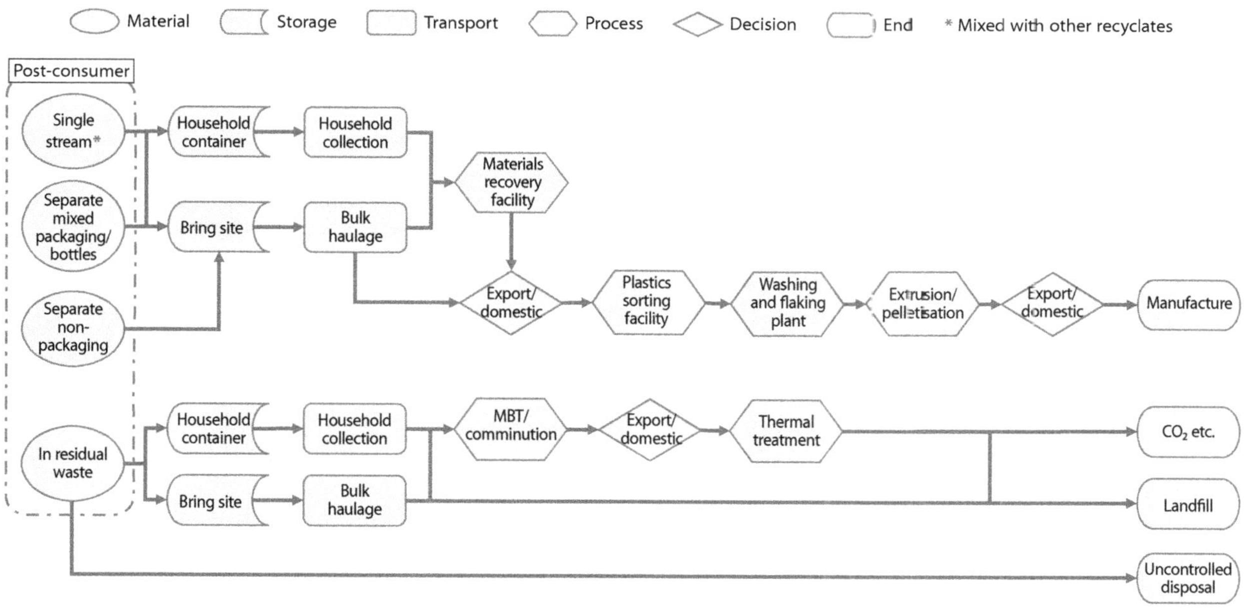

Figure 4.3. **Material flow for post-industrial plastics**

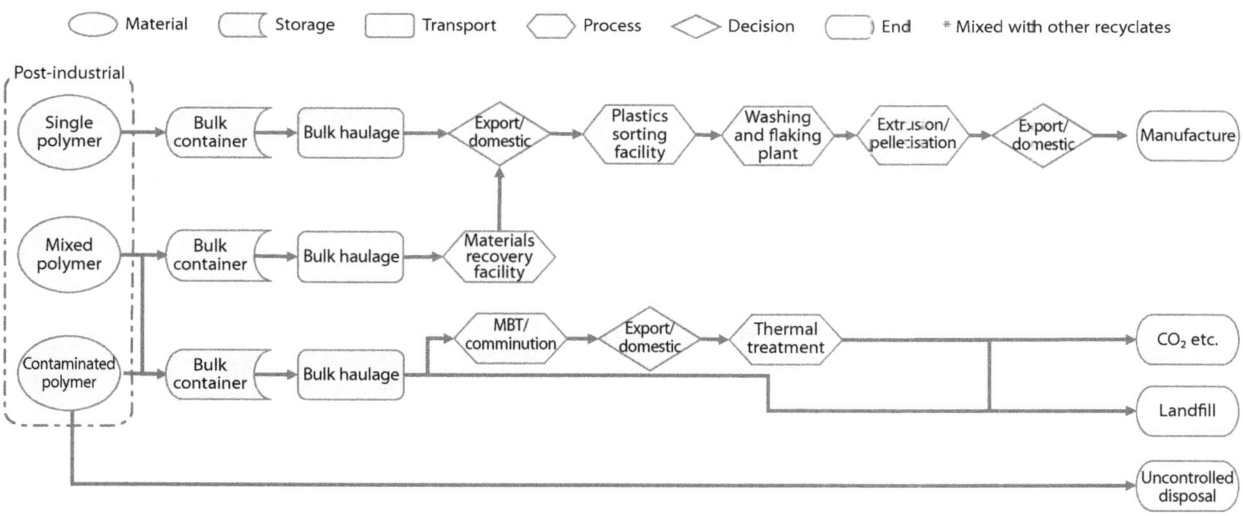

4.3. Primary sorting of waste plastics

4.3.1. Primary sorting technology for waste plastics

Regardless of the system used to collect plastics, some degree of sorting will usually be necessary to prepare a product that is suitable for recycling. Sorting can be broadly divided into positive picking (removing the target material from non-target materials), and negative picking (removing non-target materials from the target). A selection of commonly used sorting technologies are summarised in Table 4.2. Other plastics identification methods include: tribo-electric separation, magnetic density separation, laser introduced break down spectroscopy, and hyper spectral imaging (HSI) (Singh et al., 2017[44]).

Table 4.2. **Summary of sorting methods for separating different polymer types and colours**

Sorting type	Description of process	Prevalence
Manual	Materials are sorted positively or negatively by people either from a static surface, conveyer belt, or in very low-income countries, from the floor or dumpsite.	Predominantly in low and middle-income countries, but also, to some degree in advanced mechanical plants for negative picking (removal of contaminants). Issues around worker's safety, rights and welfare.
Induction sorting	Inductive sensors detect metals which are positively from other materials via fast air jets ("air knives").	Uncommon.
Eddy current	Counter-rotating magnetic field repels non-ferrous metals; positively selecting them from other materials	Very common.
Drum separator (trommel)/screen	Separates material via particle size. Perforated drum or screen causes smaller particles to fall whilst larger particles remain in the drum.	Very common.
Sink-float separation	Separation of plastics based on specific weight – often in water where PET, PVC, and PS will sink and PE, PP, and EPS will float.	Very common in middle and high-income countries.
X-ray (Bruno, 2000[45])	X-rays are directed at the material, which cause a unique peak in the x-ray spectrum which is detected by a camera, which is connected to an air jet,and positively selecting the materials being detected.	Useful for sorting very dirty bottles or those with large labels as it can detect through, reducing in use in favour of Near infra-red
Near infra-red (NIR)	Light shined on materials which are detected by camera based on the way the reflect that light in the NIR spectrum.	One of the most common sorting technologies used in high and, increasingly, middle-income countries. One of the drawbacks of this technology is its inability to identify black plastics against the background of a similarly coloured conveyer belt. This is a subject of much debate in Europe and has led to several attempts to intervene in the market to encourage manufacturers to either stop making it or include additives to make the plastics detectable (Waste Management World, 2017[46]).

Source: Worrell and Reuter (2014[44]), *Handbook of Recycling: State-of-the-art for practitioners, analysts and scientists*, http://bit.ly/2xO4SNt.

Mechanical sorting technology for waste plastics has improved significantly in the last few decades. Most recently, improvements in the efficacy of optical sorting technology have increased the viability of the market for recycled plastics. That said, material streams continue to suffer from high contamination rates. In the UK, which has a mixture of advanced and manual MRF technology, the average efficiency of plastics sorting results in output material which is 10% contaminated (WRAP, 2017[47]). This level of contamination increases the pressure on downstream plastics recyclers, who bear the costs of removing non-target materials and their further treatment or disposal.

4.3.2. Structure of the primary sorting industry for waste plastics

As discussed in Section 4.1, many of the firms operating in the recycled plastics supply chain undertake multiple activities. Cross-country data on the numbers of stakeholders undertaking sorting and recycling activities is scant – an example from the UK is provided here.

There are approximately 120 material recovery facilities (MRFs) in the United Kingdom, of which around 100 are in England. These plants range from very basic manual sort lines with nothing more than a conveyor belt, to highly complex arrays that process many thousands of tonnes of material per year. These plants accept material which has been collected mixed from household and commercial sources. The plastics they process are entirely packaging; non-packaging material would be considered a reject. More than 80% of England's MRFs produce less than 5 000 tpa of plastics, with just a handful of very large facilities operating (see Table 4.3).

Table 4.3. **Size distribution of MRFs in England and the US based on output of sorted plastics**

	Number of MRFs	
MRF output (tonnes of plastics)	**England**	**US**
<1 000	44	691
1 000-5 000	40	
5 000-10 000	12	
>10 000	6	45

Data from other nations is scant. In the United States, there were 797 MRFs operating in 2014 (US EPA, 2014[60]). Data published this year quantified the size of these plants which, on a population basis (5:1 US to UK ratio), mirrors the UK situation. There has been a gradual move in recent years towards construction of larger regional MRFs and the reduction in the number of smaller, dual stream MRFs.

Not included in the above calculations are plastics recovery facilities (PRFs). The definition of PRFs varies, but the term can be used to describe plants that carry out a high degree of plastic sorting (i.e. separating plastics into different polymer types), but that stop short of shredding, flaking and washing. There are possibly 4-5 of these plants in the UK at present; a list and description can be found in Annex K.

4.4. Recycling waste plastics

The following sections provide an overview of the stages involved in plastics reprocessing. It should be noted that there is significant variation in process types according to the material being processed and the product output specification. A summary is provided here which is also depicted graphically in Figures 4.4 and 4.5.

4.4.1. Mechanical recycling

4.4.1.1. Mechanical recycling of thermoplastics

Mechanical recycling is the predominant technology for recycling plastics and is carried out in four general stages (Figure 4.4).

Figure 4.4. **Mechanical plastics recycling stages**

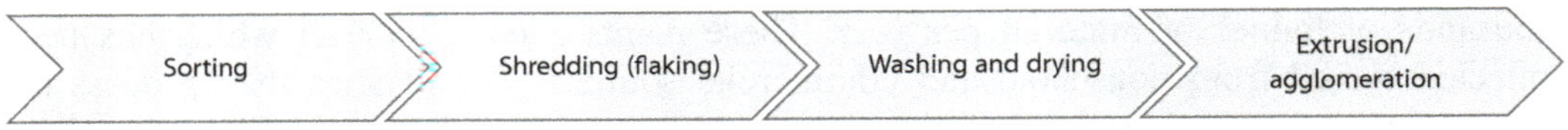

Once in a plastics recycling plant, materials undergo a pre-sorting operation, using the same technologies shown in Table 4.2. The duplication of process is somewhat surprising, but is common with all recyclate material types. There have been improvements in the efficiency of primary processing, however it is limited in its capability to produce very pure material streams. Furthermore, material sorters often try to increase utilisation of high capital equipment by processing greater quantities, which lowers accuracy. The consistency and quality of input materials also impacts significantly on the cost of operations as poorer quality material requires more effort to purify and increases the cost of disposing of rejected material (Zia, Bhatti and Ahmad Bhatti, 2007[48]).

Economic barrier: Recycled plastics re-processors have limited control over the quality of their input materials which burdens them with additional costs for sorting and disposal and treatment of rejects.

Following pre-sorting, the (mainly) singular polymer material is comminuted to reduce particle size, and thus enable further processing. This is usually done in a cutting mill which consists of counter-rotating – and sometimes also fixed – blades driven by an electric motor. A perforated plate or grill selects particle size.

After plastics have been shredded, the “flakes” are washed in either cold or hot (60°C) water to remove impurities such as food residues, labels, and dirt. Cold washing often includes the use of chemicals such as sodium hydroxide and also mechanical agitation to liberate adhered contraries.[1] The plastics are then dried to 0.1% water content before reprocessing.

There are a number of techniques for reprocessing, the two most common being agglomeration and extrusion. Agglomeration aims to increase material density to prepare material for extrusion. The process is usually used for films whereby the materials are cut into pieces, heated by friction and stuck together in “crumbs” or “agglomerates” which fall into water for cooling. Energy usage for this process is high (typically 300-700 kWh/t) and is thus often avoided.

Extrusion is by far the most common process used for recycled plastics. Recycled plastics flakes or agglomerates are blended together, sometimes with additives and/or virgin polymer and then fed into a heated (200-275°C) chamber via a hopper. A screw pushes the material forwards and it is forced through a perforated plate (die) into spaghetti like lengths which are chopped into beads which fall into water to be cooled. These are known as pellets; the processing sometimes being referred to as pelletisation.

Figure 4.5. **Detailed plastics recycling process for post-consumer bottles**

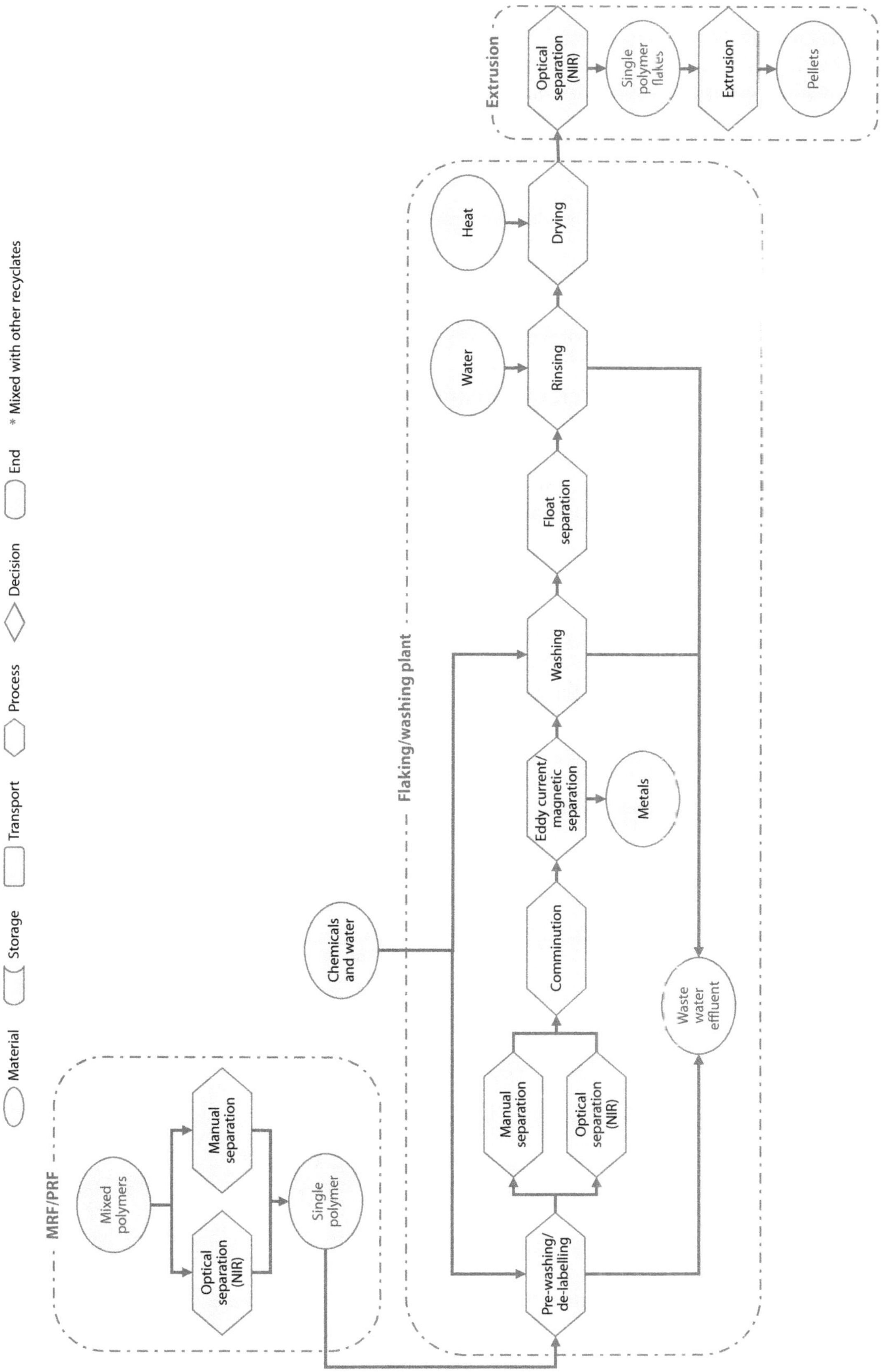

At this stage the "recycling" process is complete as the material has reached a state where it resembles the virgin product and is distinct and marketable; the plastics are equivalent to "starting materials" described in Section 3.1. The material can be described as having "end-of-waste" status – it is ready for making new plastic products via processes such as injection moulding, blow moulding, film blowing, or fibre extrusion.

4.4.1.2. Mechanical recycling of thermosets

Although global plastics production is dominated by thermoplastics, thermosets are still significant. For example, polyurethane (PU) production is approximately 28 Mtpa, of which 18 Mt becomes waste each year. As discussed in Section 2.2.2, thermoset plastics are, by their nature, difficult to recycle due to their durable properties. Since they can't be melted down and reformed, processes must either involve chemical reagents, or comminution and binding together of the particles.

The most common example of thermoset recycling is for PU which can be processed in a number of different ways (Smithers Rapara,(n.d.)[49]; American Chemistry,(n.d.)[50]; Zia, Bhatti and Ahmad Bhatti, 2007[48]):

- Re-bonded flexible foam can be granulated, mixed with adhesive and pressed into sheets to make carpet underlay and sports matting (see process flow in Figure 4.6);
- Post-industrial polyurethane trimmings can be finely reground or finely powdered and mixed with virgin material to create new foam or reaction injection moulded (RIM) parts;
- Adhesive pressing or particle bonding involves mixing finely ground polyurethane parts from automobiles, refrigerators or industrial trim with very strong binding agents. Under heat, the resultant material is pressed into boards and mouldings, often with very high recycled content; and
- Compression moulding can be used to create 100% recycled products by taking finely ground RIM and reinforced RIM Chemical Recycling parts and applying high pressure and heat in a mould.

Figure 4.6. **Schematic for flexible PU foam re-bonding**

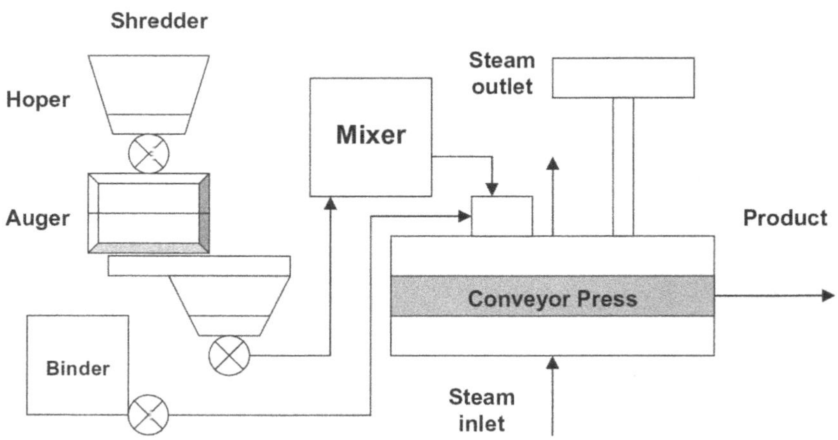

Source: Al-Salem, Lettieri and Baeyens (2009[64]), *Recycling and recovery routes of plastic solid waste (PSW): A review*, http://bit.ly/2uC9M3A.

Another example of thermoset recycling, for which it is claimed that there has been some success, involves cross-linked polyethylene (commonly used for cable jacketing). Whilst this cannot be recycled as is due to the crosslinking, it can be mixed with 40% virgin non-crosslinked PE (the thermoplastic variety) to produce a material with good mechanical properties for use in injection moulding applications.

Technical barrier: Technologies for recycling thermosets are limited (Fiberline Composites, 2010[51]).

4.4.1.3. Structure of the mechanical plastics recycling industry

Limited cross-country data exists on the structure of the plastics recycling industry. The information presented below has been developed on the basis of the questionnaires issued by the OECD along with some additional sources (see Table. 4.4).

Table 4.4. **Comparison of plastics recycling businesses across selected countries**

Country	Number of plastics waste recyclers	Amount of plastics processed (tpa)	Mean processed per company (tpa)
China	25 000	24 500 000	980
Poland	324	1 315 841	4 061
Austria	35	330 000	9 429
USA (HDPE bottle processors only)	28	466 929	16 676
UK (includes dedicated sorters)	40	1 300 000	32 500

Source: data on UK plastic waste recyclers: UK Environment Agency (2017[49]), *National Packaging Waste Database*, http://bit.ly/2y5jXOO; UK Environment Agency (2017[50]), *Waste Data Interrogator*, http://bit.ly/2hU0ZnV; data on UK amount of plastics processed: Data Gov (2017[51]), *UK Statistics on Waste*, http://bit.ly/2xmU1tN.

Available data suggest that countries with higher per-capita incomes, such as the UK and US, operate recycling plants with much greater capacity than lower income countries such as Poland and China. Austria is a slight anomaly as it has relatively high income levels, but operates smaller plants. This may be in proportion to the country's size but there is a risk of aggregating and simplifying data from a complex industry because all plants are different. A more detailed summary of Austria's plastics recycling business in Table 4.5 shows that in fact Austria has a range of different plastics recycling plants. Data from the United States also indicates the existence of different plant sizes (Table 4.6).

Table 4.5. **Summary of plastics recycling facilities in Austria by type of process**

Type of plant	Number of plastics waste recyclers	Amount of plastics processed (tpa)	Mean processed per company (tpa)
Grinding plants	15	50 000	3 333
PET recycling	3	80 000	26 667
Polyolefins	7	150 000	21 429
Post-industrial	10	50 000	5 000
Totals	**35**	**330 000**	**9 429**

Table 4.6. **Summary of HDPE recycling facilities in the US**

Size of plant (tpa)	Number of HDPE waste recycling plants	Amount of HDPE processed (tpa)	Mean plant size (tpa)
<4 500	13	29 484	2 268
4 500-13 500	7	75 296	10 757
>13 500	8	361 967	45 246
Total	**28**	**466 747**	

It is important to note that there is considerable uncertainty in available capacity. For instance, the permitted capacity of UK waste sites is approximately 1.2 million tpa. However, WRAP reports that the total capacity of re-processors is approximately 600 000 tpa (WRAP, 2016[52]). The shortfall could be related to the difference between utilisation rate and maximum authorised capacity, but it may also be because the definition of a plastics recycler is different in different datasets.

In comparison to the primary plastics industry (see Section 2.2), the recycled plastics industry is clearly smaller and more fragmented. The economies of scale commanded by the primary plastics industry combined with the maturity of the market, places primary plastics producers in a considerably stronger position in the market compared to recycled plastics producers.

Economic barrier: Compared to the primary plastics market, plastics re-processors (even in high-income countries) are small and fragile and, as a result, vulnerable to market shocks.

4.4.2. Chemical recycling

Chemical recycling refers to technological processes that convert polymers into their constituent molecules, which can then be used as feedstock for new plastics, fuels or other petrochemicals (Al-Salem, Lettieri and Baeyens, 2009[53]). Many of the chemical recycling technologies are still at research stage (see Table 4.7 for a summary). They require consistent feedstocks, which are not always forthcoming in the market for recycled plastics and, when they are, are typically processed using mechanical recycling. However, chemical recycling represents a potential solution to the challenges associated with mixed and contaminated plastics waste streams, and could also potentially be used for recycling thermoset plastics, for which there are limited commercially viable options.

One of the main advantages of chemical recycling is that they have the potential to treat contaminated and heterogeneous mixtures of polymers with only limited pre-treatment. Conversely, many of the processes produce fuels which, when combusted, contribute to global warming as the raw materials are derived from fossil carbon sources (Haig et al., 2013[54]).

Technical barrier: Chemical recycling has not yet been demonstrated to be commercially viable for recycling post-consumer plastics waste.

Some commercial scale pyrolysis and gasification plants have been constructed and others are reportedly under construction. However, these technologies have not yet entered mainstream application and are still considered to be fairly marginal. However, it is relatively well-established, albeit at a small level, in Japan.

Table 4.7. **Summary of chemical recycling types**

Chemical processing type	Specific technology	Description of process	Technological readiness
Thermolysis	Pyrolysis (thermal cracking)	Thermal degradation (500-800oC) in the absence of oxygen (same process as charcoal making)/ inert atmosphere. Produces a carbonised char, syngas and liquid hydrocarbon oils.	Struggling to achieve viability at commercial level due to instability-contamination issues.
	Gasification	Partial oxygenation at high temperatures. Dried, mechanically sorted plastics are granulated to optimum size particle and gasified in reaction chamber to produce high calorific value syngas (CO & H) and char (can be either combusted directly or used to synthesise products such as methanol or ammonia).	Promising emerging technology that has had limited success at commercial scale to date.
	Liquid-gas hydrogenation	Addition of hydrogen via chemical reaction, forming highly saturated fuel products.	Expensive as it relies on supply of pure hydrogen and very high pressures; most processes thought to be at max. TR3 stage.
Chemical depolymerisation	Methanolysis	Degradation of PET to dimethyl terephthalate.	High cost associated with the separation and refining of the mixture – process sometimes unstable – not used commercially.
	Glycolysis	Uses ethylene glycol to produce bis (2-hydroxyethyl) terephthalate (in case of PET) and other PET glycolyzates; used for manufacture of copolyesters, hydrophobic dyestuffs, unsaturated resins, polyurethane foams, and acrylic coatings.	Least capital-intensive process – oldest and simplest.
	Hydrolysis	Heated with an excess of water at high temperatures.	Products can be used to produce virgin PET, or may be converted to (expensive) chemicals like oxalic acid – slow and expensive.
	Ammonolysis	As hydrolysis with ammonia.	Not commercially used.

Source: Adapted from Beyene 2014[54], *Recycling of plastic waste into fuels, a review*, http://bit.ly/2wX0Mme; Bartolome et al. 2012[55], *Recent Developments in the Chemical Recycling of PET*, http://bit.ly/2w8RxlS; Al-Salem, Lettieri and Baeyens, 2009[52], *Recycling and recovery routes of plastic solid waste (PSW): A review*, http://bit.ly/2uC9M3A; Worrell and Reuter, 2014[54],), *Handbook of Recycling: State-of-the-art for practitioners, analysts and scientists*, http://bit.ly/2xO4SNt; Butler, Devlin and McDonnell (2011[51]), *Waste Polyolefins to Liquid Fuels via Pyrolysis: Review of Commercial State-of-the-Art and Recent Laboratory Research*, http://bit.ly/2w8XEGW.

Note

1. The washing step may be skipped entirely if the plastics originate from a post-industrial source or one where the composition can be reliably assumed not to affect further reprocessing or use.

References

Al-Salem, S., P. Lettieri and J. Baeyens (2009), "Recycling and recovery routes of plastic solid waste (PSW): A review", *Waste Management*, Vol. 29/10, pp. 2625-2643, http://dx.doi.org/10.1016/J.WASMAN.2009.06.004. [53]

American Chemistry((n.d.)), *Polyurethane Recycling*, https://polyurethane.americanchemistry.com/Polyurethane-Recycling/(accessed on 26 March 2018). [50]

Anderson, J. (2015), "ATH use in flame retardants: An overview of the industry and growth in Asia", *Roskill*, https://www.metalbulletin.com/events/download.ashx/document/speaker/8449/a0ID000000X0j5MMAR/Presentation (accessed on 27 March 2018). [83]

Bartolome, L. et al. (2012), "Recent Developments in the Chemical Recycling of PET", http://cdn.intechopen.com/pdfs/32561/InTech-Recent…recycling_of_pet.pdf (accessed on 26 March 2018). [98]

Beyene, H. (2014), "Recycling of plastic waste into fuels, a review", *International Journal of Science Technology and Society*, Vol. 2/6, pp. 190-195, http://dx.doi.org/10.11648/j.ijsts.20140206.15. [97]

Bruno, E. (2000), "Automated Sorting of Plastics for Recycling", https://pdfs.semanticscholar.org/e6e5/110c06f67171409bab3b38f742db6dc110fc.pdf (accessed on 26 March 2018). [45]

Butler, E., G. Devlin and K. McDonnell (2011), "Waste Polyolefins to Liquid Fuels via Pyrolysis: Review of Commercial State-of-the-Art and Recent Laboratory Research", *Waste and Biomass Valorization*, Vol. 2/3, pp. 227-255, http://dx.doi.org/10.1007/s12649-011-9067-5. [99]

Data Gov (2017), *UK Statistics on Waste*, https://data.gov.uk/dataset/uk_statistics_on_waste (accessed on 26 March 2018). [96]

EUROPEN (2009), "Modern Beverage Container Policy", www.embopar.pt/folder/documento/81_2009%20Modern%20Beverage%20Container%20Policy.pdf (accessed on 26 March 2018). [41]

Fiberline Composites (2010), *Breakthrough: Recycling of fibreglass is now a reality* |, https://fiberline.com/news/miljoe/breakthrough-recycling-fibreglass-now-reality (accessed on 28 March 2018). [51]

GIZ (2013), "Operator Models. Respecting Diversity Concepts for Sustainable Waste Management", https://www.giz.de/en/downloads/giz2013-swm-operator-models-sourcebook-en.pdf (accessed on 26 March 2018). [39]

IIED (2016), "Informality and inclusive green growth", www.iied.org (accessed on 26 March 2018). [43]

OECD (2013), "Waste Management Services", www.oecd.org/daf/competition/Waste-management-services-2013.pdf (accessed on 26 March 2018). [38]

Pro Europe((n.d.)), *Packaging waste legislation in Denmark*, www.pro-e.org/Denmark (accessed on 26 March 2018). [42]

Singh, N. et al. (2017), "Recycling of plastic solid waste: A state of art review and future applications", *Composites Part B: Engineering*, Vol. 115, pp. 409-422, http://dx.doi.org/10.1016/j.compositesb.2016.09.013. [44]

Smithers Rapara((n.d.)), "Brief Review of the Methods of Recycling of Polyurethane Foam Wastes", https://www.smithersrapra.com/SmithersRapra/media/Sample-Chapters/Recycling-of-Polyurethane-Wastes.pdf (accessed on 26 March 2018). [49]

U.S. Environmental Protection Agency (2011), *Marine Debris in the North Pacific*, https://nepis.epa.gov/Exe/ZyNET.exe/P100CYAN.TXT?ZyActionD=ZyDocument&Client=EPA&Index=2011+Thru+2015&Docs=&Query=&Time=&EndTime=&SearchMethod=1&TocRestrict=n&Toc=&TocEntry=&QField=&QFieldYear=&QFieldMonth=&QFieldDay=&IntQFieldOp=0&ExtQFieldOp=0&XmlQuery= (accessed on 23 March 2018). [88]

UK Environment Agency (2017), "National Packaging Waste Database", https://npwd.environment-agency.gov.uk/Public/PublicReports.aspx (accessed on 26 March 2018). [94]

UK Environment Agency (2017), *Waste Data Interrogator*, https://data.gov.uk/dataset/waste-data-interrogator-2014 (accessed on 26 March 2018). [95]

Villanueva, A. and P. Eder (2014), "End-of-waste criteria for waste plastic for conversion", *European Commission: JRC Technical Reports*, http://publications.jrc.ec.europa.eu/repository/bitstream/111111111/33010/1/2014-jrc91637%20.pdf (accessed on 26 March 2018). [14]

Waste Management World (2017), "Roadmap to Better Recycling for Black Plastics Launched", https://waste-management-world.com/a/roadmap-to-better-recycling-for-black-plastics-launched (accessed on 26 March 2018). [46]

WasteAid (2017), *Making Waste Work: Community waste management toolkit*, https://wasteaid.org.uk/toolkit/ (accessed on 26 March 2018). [40]

Worrell, E. and M. Reuter (2014), *Handbook of recycling : state-of-the-art for practitioners, analysts, and scientists*, Elsevier, https://books.google.co.uk/books?id=gQfUAgAAQBAJ&printsec=frontcover&source=gbs_ge_summary_r&cad=0#v=onepage&q&f=false (accessed on 26 March 2018). [92]

WRAP (2017), *Materials Pricing Report*, www.wrap.org.uk/content/materials-pricing-report (accessed on 26 March 2018). [9]

Zia, K., H. Bhatti and I. Ahmad Bhatti (2007), "Methods for polyurethane and polyurethane composites, recycling and recovery: A review", *Reactive and Functional Polymers*, Vol. 67/8, pp. 675-692, http://dx.doi.org/10.1016/J.REACTFUNCTPOLYM.2007.05.004. [48]

Chapter 5

Markets and trade in waste plastics

This chapter focusses on markets for waste and recycled plastics. It begins with a stocktake of the key sources of information regarding trade in waste plastics, and notes that trade volumes represent a relatively small proportion (around 4%) of overall plastic waste generation. The major exporters and importers of plastics waste are then discussed alongside the potential implications of recent Chinese restrictions on the import of plastics waste. The chapter concludes with a discussion of the key factors that govern the competitiveness of secondary plastics. Four key factors are identified: the price of virgin plastics (those derived from fossil fuel inputs), the cost of supplying secondary sourced resin, the demand for recycled plastics, and the availability of alternative waste management options.

5.1. Data sources

Data concerning trade in waste plastics can be divided into two broad groups according to the way the data is collected:

- **International trade data** provides information on the physical volume and cost of materials traded between nations. This is provided in customs declarations and collated at national level.
- **Industry surveys** collect data from stakeholders in the waste plastics business on the prices paid or received at a particular point in time; these are published in public or members only indices

The following sections look at these sources in detail.

5.1.1. International trade data

5.1.1.1. Material classification conventions

Two main classification systems are used to track global trade and hence waste plastics data. The Standard International Trade Classification (SITC) (United Nations, 2006[55]) codes are an international system maintained by the United Nations (UN) to standardise the collation of import and export data. The commodity groupings of SITC reflect (a) the materials used in production, (b) the processing stage, (c) market practices and uses of the products, (d) the importance of the commodities in terms of world trade, and (e) technological changes.

The Harmonised System (HS) is developed and maintained by the World Customs Organization and provides more granularity than the SITC system. The HS is organised logically by economic activity or component material.

Table 5.1. **Comparison of classification systems for waste plastics international trade**

Classification system	Section	Chapter	Heading		
Standard International Trade Classification (SITC)	57-Plastics	579-Waste plastics	5791		Waste, pairings and scrap of polymers of ethylene
			5792		Waste, pairings and scrap of Polymers of styrene
			5793		Waste, pairings and scrap of Polymers of vinyl chloride
			5799		Waste, pairings and scrap of Other plastics
Harmonised system (HS)	39-Plastics	3915-waste, parings and scrap, of plastics	391510		Waste, Parings, Scrap of Polymers of Ethylene (including HDPE and LDPE)
			391520		Waste, Parings, Scrap of Polymers of Styrene
			391530		Waste, Parings, Scrap of Polymers of Vinyl Chloride
			391590	3915900010	Waste, Parings, Scrap of Other Plastics: polymers of polyethylene terephthalate
				39159011	Waste, Parings, Scrap of Other Plastics: polymers of propylene

As the HS code system seems to be more commonly used international at the six digit level (rather than the eight or ten digit level). The SITC is correlated with the HS sub-headings, so that high level reporting can be done that correlates with previous UN reporting. The systems' classifications for waste plastics are compared in Table 5.1.

Finally, the Combined Nomenclature (CN), system is an EU classification that is based on the HS system described above, but contains two additional numbers to add granularity to the codes; for waste plastics however, the codes are the same.

5.1.1.2. Customs declarations

International trade data relies largely on customs declarations. These data are collated at the country level by national government agencies and submitted to centralised statistical data centres. Trade data at the country level are available from the government agencies that manage customs declarations and the collection of trade statistics (e.g. HMRC or USA Trade), but these same data are also collected at a European and Global level by the European Commission (Eurostat) and the United Nations (Comtrade) respectively. Examples of customs declaration data source are provided in Table 5.2.

Table 5.2. **Summary of international plastics trade data sources**

Dataset name	Publisher	Geographical scope		Classification system	Polymer types reported
Comtrade	UN	International	Global	HS	Waste polymers of ethylene, polymers of styrene, polymers of vinyl chloride, and "other" waste plastics
Comext	Eurostat (EC)	Regional	European trade (internal and external with non-member states)	CN	Polymers of ethylene, polymers of styrene, polymers of vinyl chloride, polymers of propylene and "other" waste plastics
Various national datasets	Examples: HMRC (UK), USA Trade Online	National	Country level	Various	Various

5.1.1.3. Calculation of trade volumes and price

Indicative prices for recycled plastics can be calculated by using the trade value of imports and exports divided by the tonnages. The resulting prices (in USD per tonne) should be viewed as averages as they do not take into account the grade of the plastics. It is important to recognise this approach can provide rather crude estimates. Imports reported by one country do not always coincide with exports reported by its trading partner. The time lag taken for countries to report their data (e.g. member States must provide Eurostat with final detailed data at the latest by October following the reference year) means that it is likely there will be missing data after the beginning of 2016. As such, at the time of writing, only datasets up until end of 2015 are available for analysis. Although Eurostat and UN Comtrade have been in existence since 1953 and 1962, data is only considered reliable from the year 2000.

5.1.1.4. Polymer-specific trade data

Customs declaration datasets do not separate polymers of ethylene into HDPE, LDPE and PE so the price calculated would only be the average price of polymers of ethylene. Neither of these datasets separate out PET, this is classified under "other waste plastics". Eurostat breaks down the waste polymers into polymers of ethylene, polymers of styrene, polymers of vinyl chloride, polymers of propylene and "other" waste plastics. Comtrade only distinguishes waste polymers of ethylene, polymers of styrene, polymers of vinyl chloride, and "other" waste plastics.

5.1.2. Surveys

Although international trade data can be used to estimate prices, this is not a particularly accurate method. As such, surveys are often used as the main data source for understanding price variations. These data are collected by organisations through surveying industry networks. The principle sources of this type identified are Plastics Information Europe (PIEWEB), Plastics News (USA), EUWID, Let's Recycle, WRAP, the CIF Ontario price sheet. Table 5.3 summarises the key sources of price data from industrial surveys.

Table 5.3. **Summary of material price indices (data obtained from surveys of material buyers and sellers)**

Dataset name	Publisher	Geographical scope	Polymer type reported
letsrecycle.com price indicators for plastics	Let's Recycle	UK domestic and export prices	• Plastics bottles: Clear and light blue PET, Coloured PET, HDPE natural, HDPE mixed colour, mixed • Plastic films: UK PE Printed, UK PP Printed, UK Clear – Natural, Export 80:20, Export 90:10, Export, 95:5, Export 98:2
Materials Pricing Report	Waste and Resources Action Programme (WRAP)	UK	• PET, HDPE, LDPE, mixed rigid plastics
Historical Resin Pricing of Recycled Plastics	Plastics News	USA	• PET, HDPE, LDPE, PS, HMWHDPE, PVC, ABS, LLDPE, PP
EUWID Markets and price trends	EUWID Recycling and Waste Management	Europe but focussed on developments in Germany, the UK, France, Italy and Poland	• Not known.
PIEWEB			• PET, HDPE, LDPE, PP
CIF Ontario Price Sheet	Reclay StewardEdge	Ontario, Canada	• PET, HDPE, LDPE, PS and PP
Plastics Information Europe Polymer Prices	Plastics Information Europe	Western Europe and China, North America and Russia	• PET, HDPE, LDPE, PP
Recycling: Weighted average price of recycled materials	Fostplus	Belgium	• HDPE and PET
Precios materiales reciclados	Anarpa	Spain	• HDPE, LDPE, PS, PP, ABS

All of these organisations record prices for PET and HDPE, most record LDPE and some record PS and PP. Plastics News also covers PVC, ABS, LLDPE, and HDPE. PIEWEB covers Europe and has the largest network of industry contacts of those listed with over more than 600 regular panel participants in Europe. It also has the longest temporal coverage, having been in existence since 1984. More details on each of the data sources are provided in Annex L.

These organisations recognise that there are potential problems with data manipulation by producer and processor contacts who might attempt to increase or decrease pricing by giving a false figure. However, most of these organisations state they have verification checks and processes to help exclude contacts giving false information. The organisations with a larger pool of contacts are more likely to have representative data, not skewed by outliers. However, this could be an issue for those organisations that often only have a handful of data suppliers. This is particularly relevant for those that cover a smaller geographical area, such as Let's Recycle, WRAP and the CIF Ontario Price sheet. The other factor which might impact this type of data is that some businesses have long-term contracts for purchasing waste plastics which will mean that although value might fluctuate the pricing remains fixed over the period of the contract.

Economic barrier: There is a lack of consistency in reporting of international trade and market survey data on recycled plastics. This reduces the ability of actors to make evidence-based decisions and interventions.

5.2. Global trade flows waste plastics

Approximately 13 Mt (or 4%) of the waste plastics that are generated each year are exported beyond their country of origin (UN, 2017[56]). The majority of plastics waste exports originate from high-income countries; the United States, Europe, and Japan account for approximately 73% of global plastics waste exports (UN, 2017[56]) (see Figure 5.1). More detailed, year-by-year data for each main exporter country is provided in Annex M.

Figure 5.1. **Top ten global exporters of waste plastics, 2006 to 2015 (excluding Hong Kong)**

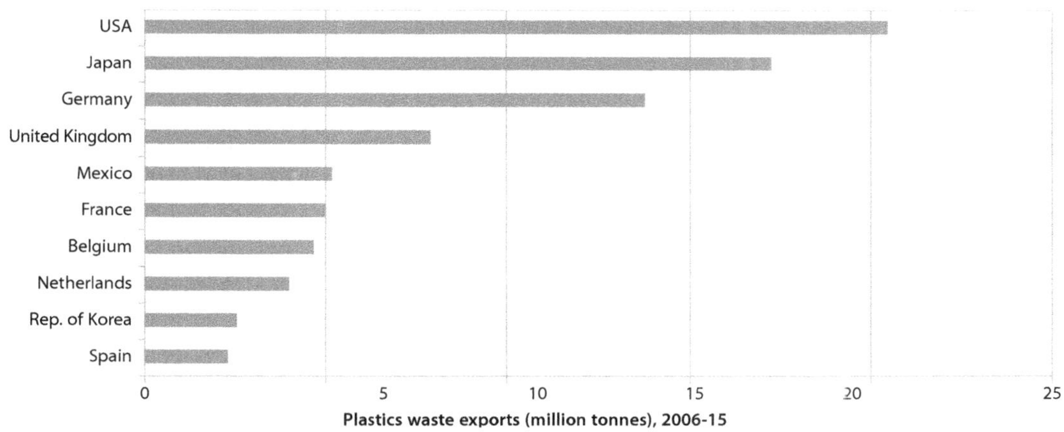

Source: Based on analysis of UN Comtrade data (2017[56]), http://bit.ly/2jL1FIk.

China has been the main destination for exported waste plastics during recent years (ISWA, 2014[33]). Taken together with Hong Kong, which re-exports the majority of the waste plastics it imports to mainland China, this market accounted for approximately two thirds of waste plastics traded globally in 2015. Other importers include the Netherlands (3.9%), Germany (3.5%) and the USA (2.6%).

Figure 5.2 illustrates changes in the quantities of waste plastic imported to China (including Hong Kong), Europe, North America and other Asian countries (excluding China and Hong Kong). Details for individual countries can be found in Annex N.

Figure 5.2. **Global waste plastics imports, 2006-15 (million tonnes)**

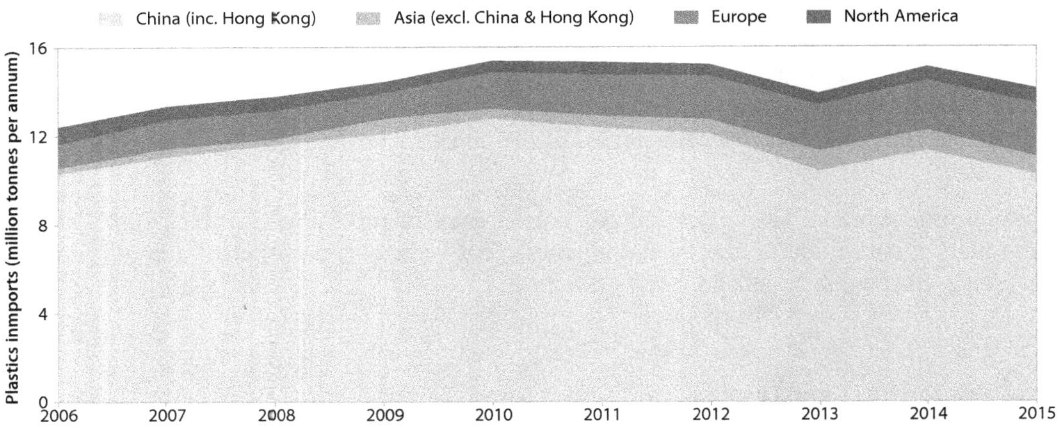

Source: Based on analysis of UN Comtrade data (2017[56]), http://bit.ly/2jL1FIk.

The quantity of waste plastics imported by China increased steadily from 2006 to 2010, and then began to level off. Imported quantities dropped significantly in 2013 as a result of the "Green Fence" import restrictions and, more recently, China's operation "National Sword" (see below for more information).

This overall reduction in Chinese waste plastics imports coupled with increasing supply of recycled plastics has created opportunities for growth of recycling markets in other regions. A number of countries in Europe (e.g. Germany, Belgium, Portugal, France and the Czech Republic), South East Asia (e.g. Malaysia and Indonesia), and Southern Asia (specifically India) have imported increasing quantities of waste plastics over recent years. More detailed analysis is required to test the hypothesis that this is building a resilient recycling sector in these countries, but it does appear that the Chinese import restrictions are creating opportunities elsewhere.

Economic barrier: Demand for recovered plastics has been dominated by a small number of countries. This makes these markets vulnerable to demand shocks.

5.3. Current and historic price trends

5.3.1. The recycled plastics value chain

The value of recycled plastics increases from the point the materials are collected through to when the material ceases to become waste ("End of Waste") (Villanueva and Eder, 2014[14]) (Box 5.1). This is usually the point at which the plastics have been cleaned sufficiently and comminuted into "flakes" which can be fed into an extruder and either moulded or turned into pellets for further extrusion or moulding.

Box 5.1. End of Waste

In the European Union, end of waste describes the point at which waste regulations no longer apply to the material. Achieving this status requires application through a legal process. Applicants must show that the resultant product meets the following criteria:

- the substance or object is commonly used for a specific purpose;
- a market or demand exists for such a substance or object;
- the substance or object fulfils the technical requirements for the specific purpose referred to in the first point and meets the existing legislation and standards applicable to products; and
- the use of the substance or object will not lead to overall adverse environmental or human health impacts.

The value of virgin plastics varies between different polymers due to the different levels of processing and the energy required to produce them. As discussed in Section 5.4, the value of the recycled materials is strongly linked with the price of equivalent virgin polymers.

Figure 5.3 shows the range of prices paid for different polymers from 2012-15 at different processing stages. The figure demonstrates the scale of opportunity that exists for stakeholders in the plastics value chain; that mixed materials can, with the correct technology and processing capability, be increased in approximate value by an order of magnitude of 10.

Figure 5.3. **Market value of major polymers (2012-15)**

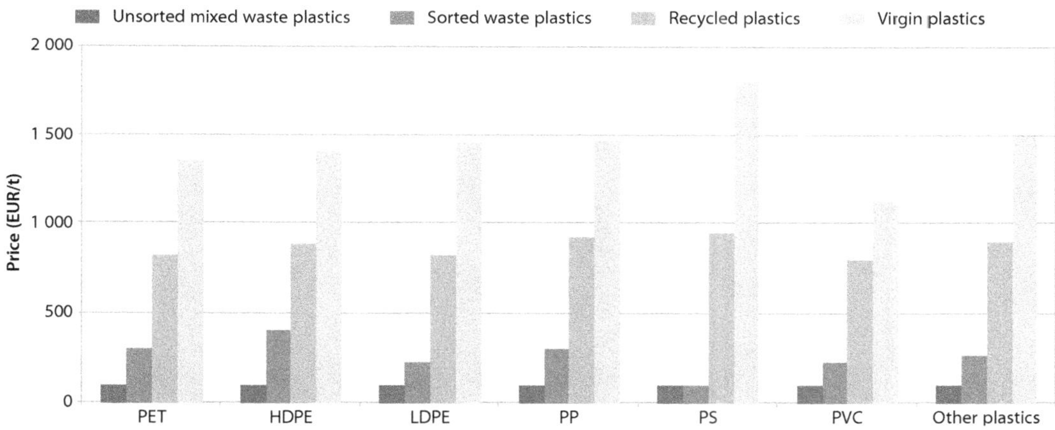

Note: Data for unsorted mixed waste plastics is from analysis of WRAP Materials Pricing Report (2012-15).

Source: OECD, based on data from Hestin, Faninger and Milios (2015[74]), *Increased EU Plastics Recycling Targets: Environmental, Economic and Social Impact Assessment*, https://bit.ly/2w7mhoM.

Descriptors are important when discussing the value of waste plastics. For instance, the price shown for "unsorted mixed waste plastics" comes from the WRAP Materials Pricing Report which is a UK index for prices (introduced in Section 5.1.2). In the report, the category is described as "mixed polymers" which is a sub-category of "plastic bottles".

However, in practice, survey respondents will be reporting prices paid for "mixed bottles", "mixed plastic containers", and "mixed plastic packaging"; each with varying composition depending on the acceptance criteria of the waste collector.

The term "sorted waste plastics" describes materials that have been separated into broad polymer types such as: Clear and light blue PET; Coloured PET; HDPE natural; and HDPE mixed colour (Jazz). As shown by the photographs in Figure 5.4 and Figure 5.5, these materials will still contain impurities such as bottle tops (often a different polymer type to the bottle), but they will be of sufficient quality that they can be further sorted and processed at a flaking and washing facility.

Figure 5.4. **Mixed colour HDPE plastic bottles, baled ready for sale as a "sorted waste plastic"**

Source: photo by Edward Cook.

Figure 5.5. **Natural HDPE plastic bottles, baled ready for sale as a "sorted waste plastic"**

Source: photo by David Lerpiniere.

It is also important to ascertain whether prices quoted are for "collected"[1] material or for material which has been "delivered" to the processor. Depending on the destination of the material and the geography of the country in which it is being traded, the difference in price can be substantial. Interviews with index survey data collectors ((n.a.), 2016[57]) ((n.a.), 2015[58]) suggest that this type of error is common amongst local authority officers that contribute to these surveys.

5.3.2. The role of China

In recent years, China has been the largest importer of plastics waste for reprocessing. Historically, much of this material has originated from ineffective sorting facilities, and has contained significant levels of contamination. Relatively weak environmental standards and enforcement coupled with low labour costs have meant that Chinese recyclers have been able to accept low quality material, negating the need for adequate separation in source countries.

In February 2013, the Chinese authorities implemented operation Green Fence. The policy aimed to improve the quality of imported waste products, and prevent the nation becoming a dumping ground for low quality materials. Green Fence increased the risk for exporters because if their products were refused at the Chinese border, the exporter would have to fund their return to the country of origin as well as finding a domestic market for the rejected material.

The immediate effects of the policy on the global plastics market were a dip in market price of trade between some developing countries and China. As the policy continued over the next three years, import checks began to take place at the point of departure, to reduce risk to exporters. In the third and final phase, entitled "Goddess of the Earth", the operation consisted mainly of carrying out checks at the point of origin.

In March 2017, the Chinese authorities announced a further crackdown on low quality waste imports called National Sword. The nine-month initiative was more stringent than Green Fence, and covered a wide range of materials, not just waste. Following this initiative (in June 2017), the authority sent out teams of thousand inspectors who reportedly visited approximately 900 plants around China; about half of the 1 792 that are licensed to import waste plastics. The Chinese Plastic Scrap Association reported that 590 were found to have breached environmental regulations and that 349 are currently under further investigation. 383 factories had their production suspended and 53 were closed completely.

In July 2017, China notified the World Trade Organisation of its intent to update its Catalogue of Solid Wastes Forbidden to Import into China. All post-consumer plastics waste was included from January 2018 (People's Republic of China,(n.d.)[59]; (n.a.),(n.d.)[60]; ISRI, 2017[61]). Finally, in November 2017, China announced its intention to amend its import quality standards GB 16487. Effective from March 2018, all imports of plastics scrap must contain no more than 0.5% non-target material. In both cases, concerns about human health and environmental damage were the stated motivation for the restrictions.

Environmental barrier: Concerns over environmental standards for recycling in emerging markets can lead to restrictions on the flow of plastics waste being imposed.

The impact of China's import restrictions on global waste markets remain uncertain, but are potentially significant. China has traditionally accounted for around two thirds of the global trade in waste plastics – reduced imports will place pressure on waste management systems in exporting countries. Not all exporters will be affected equally. Countries that previously exported large volumes of domestic plastics waste to China (Figure 5.6), and that are unable to quickly improve waste quality are most likely to be affected. In some cases, it is likely that waste management firms in exporting countries will seek new markets for their materials. This may lead to increased pressure on waste management systems in importing countries with relatively less stringent environmental regulations.

Figure 5.6. **Exports of plastics waste to China in 2016**

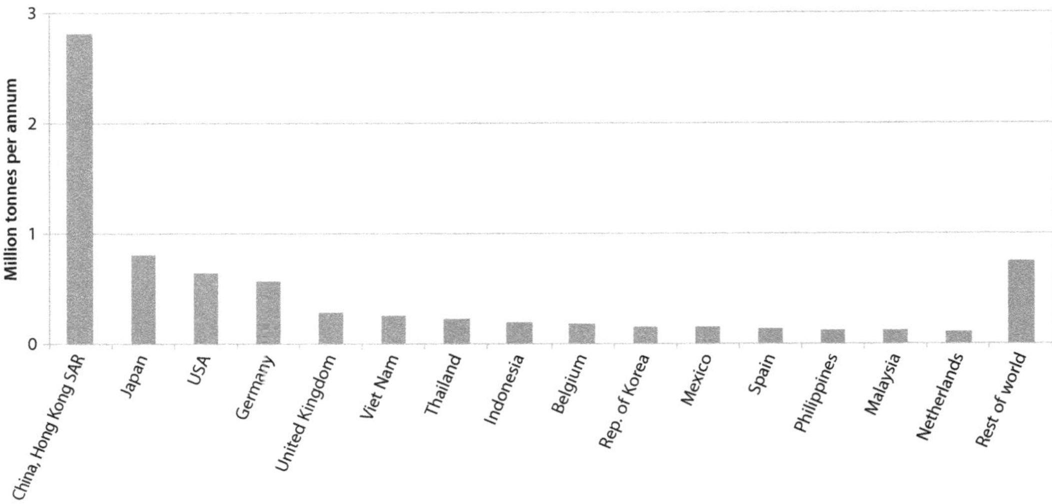

Source: Based on analysis of UN Comtrade data (2017[56]), http://bit.ly/2jL1FIk.

5.4. Price formation

The costs of collecting, sorting, and reprocessing waste plastics, and the relatively low market value of the resulting recycled plastics, are key factors behind low global recycling rates. Public policy can serve to address some of the underlying barriers, however successful intervention in plastics markets requires an understanding of how the prices of recycled plastics are formed, and how they compare to other materials such as virgin polymers or biogenic products such as paper or wood.

In this section, some of the key factors that influence the price of recycled plastics are discussed. These factors have been grouped into four broad categories: virgin polymer prices, cost of supplying secondary sourced resin, demand for recycled material, and alternative waste management options (Figure 5.7). The focus is on thermoplastics as these represent the majority of global plastics production and recycling.

Figure 5.7. **Recycled plastics price formation**

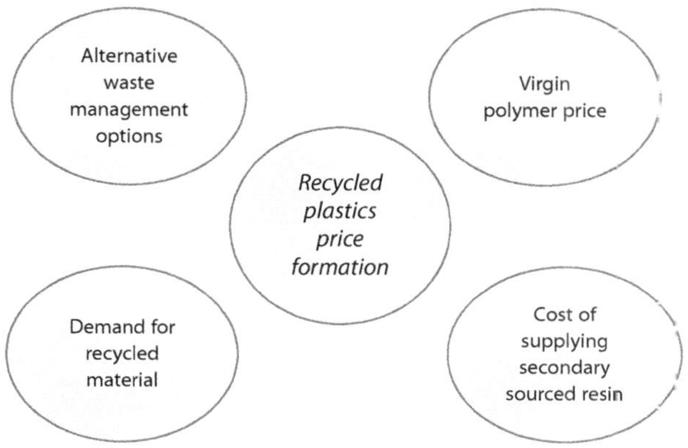

5.4.1. Virgin plastics prices

Recycled plastics prices are closely linked with their primary (virgin) equivalents. Whilst the price of oil is the strongest influence on virgin polymer prices, it is by no means the only factor, as shown in the summary of influencing factors in Table 5.4.

Table 5.4. **Summary of main factors influencing the price of virgin plastics**

Oil price	Cyclical trends
	Trader behaviour/future markets (influenced by OPEC)
	Global crises/disasters/geopolitical flash-points
	Access to future supply (i.e. reserves)
	Supply
	Demand
	Other fuel markets (e.g. shale oil – especially USA)
Grid energy price	Climate
	Season
	Fossil fuel supply and demand
	Energy policy
Cost of additives	Plasticisers/softeners (e.g. phthalates)
	Catalysts
	Flame retardants
Supply and demand for virgin plastics	Stockpiling (artificial market inflation)
	Cost of substitutes (e.g. paper, wood)
Cotton price (PET only)	Clothing market supply and demand
	Cotton quality
	Cost of substitutes (e.g. wool, plastics)
	Stockpiling (artificial inflation)

Figure 5.8 shows how the price of virgin HDPE follows the price of crude oil with a slight time-lag. Importantly, the graph also shows the impact of supply and demand by highlighting a period when the price of oil dropped considerably but the price of both

primary and recycled HDPE remained high; effectively decoupling from the oil price. This is probably due to production bottlenecks in the supply of HDPE (WRAP, 2008[62]).

Figure 5.8. **Time series comparison of HPDE with crude oil prices**

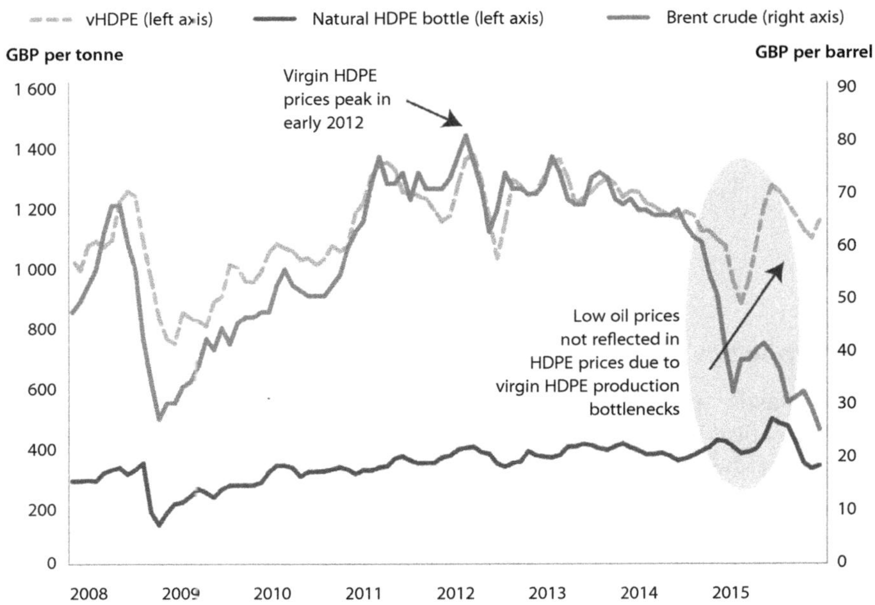

Source: WRAP (2016[51]), *Plastics Market Situation Report*, http://bit.ly/1o3IH0N.

Grid electricity prices also impact heavily on the cost of virgin plastics production. Of course, in low-middle-income countries and areas with sparse industrial geography, power generation will be localised, but the principle is the same; it takes a great deal of energy to create primary plastics. However, the price of recycled plastics is much more strongly driven by the cost of the alternative virgin polymer and less by production costs. This is one of the important factors that can determine the success of plastics recycling operations because it means that whatever the operational costs that have to be incurred by the recycling industry, their profitability is at the mercy of the cost of the virgin material which is mainly driven by oil price.

As discussed in Section 2.2.3, plastics additives make up approximately 6% by mass of virgin plastics. The cost of these is influential but less so than oil and grid electricity.

PET (also known as polyester) stands out as a slightly unusual case. Whilst the price is driven by the same factors as other plastics, it is also strongly influenced by the price of cotton. This is mainly because Chinese textile firms (one of the world's largest sources of textiles), often choose to replace the use of cotton with recycled PET when the price of cotton is high (Figure 5.9). Approximately 73% of PET recycled globally is used in the fibre industry (Bartl, 2014[63]).

Figure 5.9. **Time series comparison of global cotton and PET bottle prices**

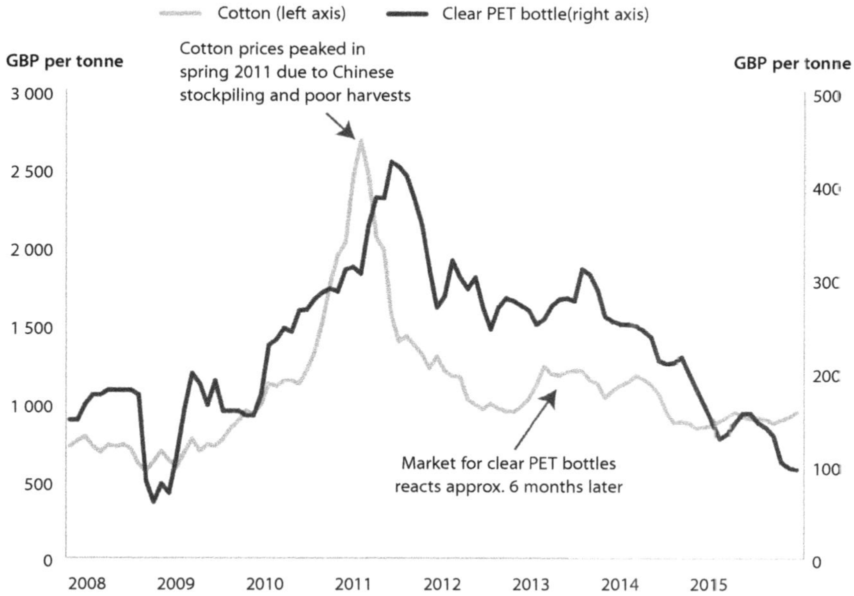

Source: WRAP (2016[51]), *Plastics Market Situation Report,* http://bit.ly/1o3IH0N.

A recent phenomenon reported by WRAP (2016[51]) is the emergence of cheaper monomer feedstock for virgin polymers (ethane as opposed to more expensive naphtha) being produced in the USA. It is not clear how this will affect the price of recycled plastics but it is likely that a decrease in value will be seen.

Economic barrier: Although demand for recycled plastics is influential in the short term, it is the price of oil and primary plastics that drive prices for recycled plastics.

5.4.2. Demand for recycled content

Market demand for recycled plastics also influences market prices, albeit to a lesser extent than demand for virgin plastics. Table 5.5 summarises some of the factors which affect demand for recycled plastics.

Table 5.5. **Summary of main factors influencing the demand for recycled content**

Consumer demand	Clothing Replacement of metal and ceramic products such as construction materials, automotive parts Competing products (wood, paper, reusable items)
Environmental policy	Producer responsibility legislation Corporate social responsibility agendas Public sector procurement policies favouring recycled content
Enabling technology	Extrusion and forming – enabling higher content of recycled material Product specification
Seasonal festivals and celebrations	Christmas Chinese New Year

Recycled plastics are generally considered to be an "imperfect substitute" (WRAP, 2007[64]) for virgin plastics. There is no differentiated market demand for their use, meaning that recycled plastics compete on the same market as their primary equivalents. In many cases, the availability and quality of recycled plastics is relatively uncertain. For manufacturing firms that use plastics as inputs, this tends to result in a preference for the use of virgin rather than recycled plastics.

Economic barrier: Lack of differentiated demand for recycled plastics.

However, in recent years, demand for recycled content has begun to increase as recycled polymer becomes a desirable product in its own right. Increasingly, consumers are demanding recycled content in packaging, creating a new corporate social responsibility agenda.

Technological innovation in extrusion and forming technology is an important factor (ISWA, 2014[33]) (Francis, Stadler and Roberts, 2016[24]). Recycled plastics do not have the same properties as virgin polymers and are usually mixed together with additives to provide the same tensile strength and ductility. For this reason, it is likely that there will always be some kind of requirement for virgin polymers. However, as innovation in extrusion and forming technology improves, a greater proportion of recycled content in products will be feasible.

Demand shocks can also have an impact on markets for recycled plastics. The recently implemented Chinese import restrictions (see Section 5.3.2) are one such example. Figure 5.10 shows the fall in waste PET prices that was associated with the implementation of Operation Green Fence.

Figure 5.10. **UK export price for mixed bottles**

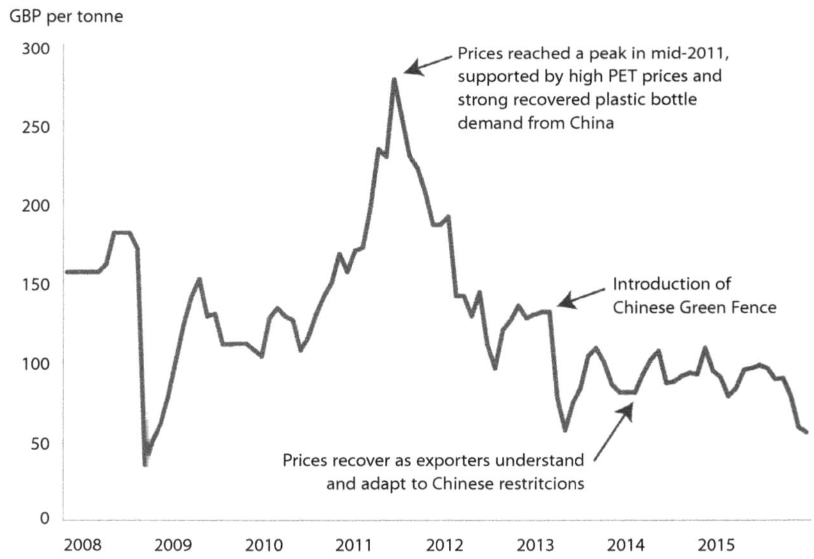

Source: WRAP (2016[51]), *Plastics Market Situation Report*, http://bit.ly/1o3IH0N.

5.4.3. Cost of supplying resin from secondary sources

The cost of recycled plastics production also affects the market for recycled plastics, and determines whether producers can stay in business or not. Factors that affect recycling costs are summarised in Table 5.6. Indicative production costs for the European Union are shown in Table 5.7.

Table 5.6. **Summary of main factors influencing the cost of supplying secondary sourced resin**

Policy	Legislation mandating weight or proportion of plastics that must be recycled (creating an economy of scale)
	Producer responsibility legislation and trading platforms
	Customs (costs of administration and procedures)
Global supply chain networks	Westbound freight costs and backloads to Asia on empty ships
Technological capability	Sorting (e.g. Near infra-red (NIR), X-ray)
	Flaking and washing
	Extrusion and forming
	Logistics
Capital expenditure	Sensor based sorting equipment
	Built infrastructure
Operational costs	Grid energy (or local energy generation in low-income countries)
	Real estate
	Labour
	Collections (local authority)
	Processing
	Logistics

Table 5.7. **Indicative operational costs for EU27 countries for treating waste plastics**

	Collection	Pre-treatment	Transport	Recycling	Energy recovery	Landfill
Operation costs (USD/t)*	181	222	2.4-18	535	89	88

* Converted from Euro to USD using an exchange rate of 1.2 USD to the EUR.

Source: Hestin, Faninger and Milios (2015[64]), *Increased EU Plastics Recycling Targets: Environmental, Economic and Social Impact Assessment*, https://bit.ly/2w7mhoM.

Technological advances have improved the economics of plastics recycling in recent years, reducing reliance on manual sorting, and in part, mitigating issues of contamination. In particular, the improved capability of sorting equipment has enabled increasing amounts of post-consumer packaging to be separated and cleaned, allowing access to higher polymer prices for re-processors. These technologies have considerable cost. Sorting facilities have been estimated to cost between USD 600 and 960 per tonne of capacity to construct (Caudron et al., 2014[65]) (based on packaging sorting facilities) and recycling (reprocessing) plants between USD 300 and 990/tonne of capacity (Hestin, Faninger and Milios, 2015[66]) (Box 5.2).

Global supply chain networks are also important. Developed economies (such as in Europe) import large volumes of goods from low- or middle-income economies (such as China), most of which are transported by sea. Consequently, there are a large number of empty ships returning to these countries that offer low cost haulage. Conversely, the cost of sending secondary polymer on westbound freight routes is higher, discouraging the flow of starting materials in that direction.

Economies of scale are also particularly important for plastics; increasing the viability of collection in areas of high population density.

Box 5.2. **Operational costs**

There is wide disparity between the spread of costs between low, middle and high-income countries (Hoornweg and Bhada-Tata, 2008[67]). Low income countries apportion 80-90% of the public waste management budget to collection systems; very little is allocated towards treatment or disposal.

Conversely, high income countries allocate as little as 10% to collection costs with a much higher proportion of budget allocated to intermediate processing. The type of collection system used has a considerable impact on costs, with large differences between single and multi-stream collection costs (WRAP, 2009[68]).

Further details on collection costs by disposal method are shown in Table 5.10.

Finally, under most jurisdictions, materials that are legally classified as waste are subject to additional waste management-specific regulatory requirements. This often results in additional cost and administration, associated with environmental permitting requirements for handling the material, for example. The definition of a material as a "waste" can also reduce its perceived value. There are also concerns in industry in Europe concerning the complexity of regulation that applies specifically to food contact applications. Clearly, regulation of the use of recycled plastics in sensitive applications, such as food, is essential but it has been suggested that the applicable legislation could be stream-lined.

Regulatory barrier: Regulatory requirements that affect materials classified as a "waste" can create additional costs for recyclers and also reduce the perceived value of the recycled material.

5.4.4. Other management options for waste plastics

Price formation for recycled plastics is partly influenced at a local level by the cost of alternative methods of treatment or disposal. A summary of the relevant drivers is shown in Table 5.8.

In a low-income economy, disposal of waste is often free and unregulated, which results in materials being disposed of to land, watercourses or by open burning. The incentive to recycle is therefore only driven by the value of the material itself, and without access to market, this is unlikely to be a strong enough driver.

Regulatory barrier: Poor enforcement against illegal disposal of wastes can undermine the market for recycled plastics.

Table 5.8. **Summary of main factors influencing the cost of other waste management options for waste plastics**

Policy	Economic instruments such as tax on landfill
	Producer responsibility
Operational costs	Transport
	Labour
Treatment or disposal	Landfill charges
	Incineration charges
	Geology

Conversely in developed economies such as Europe, governments have frequently implemented economic instruments such as taxes on the landfilling of waste materials. Other treatment and disposal options such as fluidised bed or moving grate incinerators (thermal treatment), are also expensive to operate bringing them close to landfill tax prices in developed countries. A summary of the costs of disposal and thermal treatment as well as collection costs is shown in Table 5.9.

Table 5.9. **Cost of collection and disposal of waste in different economies (USD/tonne)**

Treatment, collection or disposal option	Low-income	Lower middle-income	Upper middle-income	High-income
Collection	20-50	30-75	40-90	85-250
Sanitary landfill	10-30	15-40	25-65	40-100
Open dumping	2-8	3-10	NA	NA
Waste-to-energy incineration	NA	40-100	60-150	70-200

Note: Data are not shown for uncontrolled waste which equals approximately half of the waste generated in low income countries.

Source: Hoornweg and Bhada-Tata (2008[65]), *What a Waste: A Global Review of Solid Waste Management*, http://bit.ly/2rI6nNn.

In some countries, regardless of the implementation of economic instruments, geology can encourage recycling, and thus improving the economy of scale for plastics recycling. For instance, in Japan and Switzerland, the rocky ground makes it expensive to excavate landfill facilities. Whereas in the Netherlands, the low-lying terrain and proximity to the sea increases the risk of landfill liners being breached form the outside causing pollution of watercourses.

Many nations and trading blocs also use producer responsibility legislation which effectively obligates the material manufacturers to contribute towards the cost of collecting and processing waste plastics.

A large proportion of waste plastics are traded illegally. The illegal waste trade is estimated at USD 10-12 billion annually (ISWA, 2014[69]). This has a significant effect on plastics trade as it undermines the quality of compliant material.

> **Regulatory barrier:** Illegal trafficking of wastes can undermine the market value of legitimately traded waste plastics.

Note

1. The "ex-works" (inco)term specifically identifies the buyer as the entity that collects and transports the good from the seller's premises. However, in the waste business, materials can sometimes have a negative value, meaning that the position of the buyer and the seller can be inverted. Therefore it is not recommended to use the "ex-works" to describe "collected" material as confusion can arise when the material has negative value.

References

(n.a.) (2016), *Personal Communication.* [57]

(n.a.) (2015), *Reporter.* [58]

(n.a.)((n.d.)), "Catalogue of Solid Waste Forbidden to Import in China", http://bit.ly/2wJipJz (accessed on 26 March 2018). [60]

Bartl, A. (2014), "Moving from recycling to waste prevention: a review of barriers and enables", *Waste Management & Research*, Vol. 32/9, pp. 3-18, http://dx.doi.org/10.1177/0734242X14541986. [63]

Caudron, J. et al. (2014), "Étude prospective sur la collecte et le tri des déchets d'emballages et de papier dans le Service Public de Gestion des Déchets", www.ademe.fr/sites/default/files/assets/documents/adm00013578_etude_prospective_collecte_tri.pdf (accessed on 26 March 2018). [65]

Hestin, M., T. Faninger and L. Milios (2015), "Increased EU Plastics Recycling Targets: Environmental, Economic and Social Impact Assessment Final Report Prepared for Plastic Recyclers Europe", *Deloitte*, https://www2.deloitte.com/fr/fr/pages/sustainability-services/articles/increased-eu-plastics-recycling-targets-environmental-economic-and-social-impact-assessment.html (accessed on 26 March 2018). [66]

Hoornweg, D., P. Bhada-Tata and C. Kennedy (2015), "Peak Waste: When Is It Likely to Occur?", *Journal of Industrial Ecology*, Vol. 19/1, pp. 117-128, http://dx.doi.org/10.1111/jiec.12165. [31]

ISRI (2017), "Statement of the Institute of Scrap Recycling Industries", www.isri.org/docs/default-source/default-document-library/isri-comments-to-the-wto-re-notification-gtbtnchn1211-august-18-2017.pdf?sfvrsn=2 (accessed on 26 March 2018). [61]

ISWA (2014), "Waste Trafficking, Challenges and Actions to be Taken", http://bit.ly/2yvwSrj (accessed on 26 March 2018). [69]

People's Republic of China((n.d.)), "Notification to the World Trade Organisation in accordance with Article 10.6", http://bit.ly/2wJipJz (accessed on 26 March 2018). [59]

UN (2017), *Comtrade Database*, https://comtrade.un.org/ (accessed on 26 March 2018). [56]

United Nations (2006), *Standard International Trade Classification*, https://unstats.un.org/unsd/cr/registry/regcst.asp?Cl=27 (accessed on 27 March 2018). [55]

WRAP (2017), *Materials Pricing Report*, www.wrap.org.uk/content/materials-pricing-report (accessed on 26 March 2018). [9]

WRAP (2009), "Choosing the Right Recycling Collection System", www.wrap.org.uk/sites/files/wrap/Choosing%20the%20right%20recycling%20collection%20system.pdf (accessed on 26 March 2018). [68]

WRAP (2008), "The determinants of recovered plastics prices in the UK", www.wrap.org.uk/sites/files/wrap/The%20determinants%20of%20recovered%20plastics%20prices%20-%20Final.pdf (accessed on 26 March 2018). [62]

WRAP (2007), "Market Situation Report", www.wrap.org.uk/sites/files/wrap/PlasticsMktRep.pdf (accessed on 26 March 2018). [64]

Chapter 6

Barriers and interventions

This chapter synthesises the barriers that hinder more widespread plastics recycling, and offers a set of policy interventions that could help to address them. Barriers are divided into four categories: economic (such as the high cost of collecting, sorting, and reprocessing waste plastics), technical (such as the limited availability of technologies for recycling thermoset plastics), environmental (such as uncertainties about the presence of hazardous additives in plastics waste that can hinder the use of recycled plastics in certain applications), and regulatory (such as the uncontrolled dumping and burning of waste that takes place in some countries). Potential policy interventions are then presented and ranked according to how feasible and effective they are likely to be.

6.1. Barriers to plastics recycling

If recycling is to become the dominant management route for waste plastics and plastics continue to be widely used, strong and stable markets for these materials will be essential. However, these markets currently face some significant challenges, including:

- Economic challenges associated with vulnerable markets for recycled plastics and the costs of supplying resin sourced from waste plastics;
- Technical challenges associated with the wide variety of polymers and additives used, the significant levels of contamination in post-consumer waste plastics, and the practical challenges associated with collecting waste plastics;
- Environmental challenges due to the presence of hazardous additives in some waste plastics; and
- Regulatory challenges, principally associated with illegal waste trade but also due to constraints posed by existing regulation and, in low income contexts, uncontrolled dumping and burning of wastes.

The barriers identified in this report are discussed in more detail below.

6.1.1. Economic barriers

This report identified the following key economic barriers to plastics recycling:

1. **Costs of collecting, sorting and processing waste plastics are high.** This is due to several factors:
   a. **The widely distributed and diverse nature of sources of plastics waste.** Furthermore, the collection of plastics in low income countries is also limited by compaction capability. Even with sufficient markets, the amount of air which exists in packaging can often make the cost of transport prohibitive for small operators who do not have compaction equipment.
   b. **The combination of polymers of different types makes their separation for recycling difficult and costly.** Whilst collection systems for post-consumer PET and HDPE are well-established in many countries, the diversity of plastics used limits the economies of scale that are available for other less-common polymers (i.e. if the quantity of an individual polymer type is relatively low then there is less incentive to separate it).
   c. **Contamination of post-consumer plastics.** Post-consumer plastics commonly contain non-recyclable and non-target materials. This leads to materials being rejected for recycling and increases the processing costs to remove contamination. In particular, this issue affects re-processors who have limited control over the quality of their input materials.
2. **Limited resilience of the sector to market shocks.** Domestic recycling industries in regions with the highest production of plastics waste (North American and European countries) are small and fragile. Re-processors are particularly vulnerable to both market instability downstream and poor quality input material upstream, neither of which they have much control over. This represents a critical bottleneck in the recycled plastics industry. For example, several plastics recyclers have gone out of business in the UK over the last decade as a result of price falls caused by declining virgin polymer prices.

3. **The global market for plastics waste has been concentrated in small number of countries**. For example, China has accounted for roughly two thirds of waste plastics imports during the last decade. This makes markets for recycled plastics relatively vulnerable and slow to adjust to different types of demand shocks.

4. **Lack of differentiated demand for recycled plastics**, as differentiated from primary plastics. Recycled plastics are generally treated as a replacement material for primary plastics. Although demand for recycled plastics is influential in the short term, it is the price of oil and primary plastics price that drive prices for recycled plastics.

5. **Poor data on the plastics recycling sector**. Data on the generation and fate of waste plastics is limited and of poor quality. There is also limited information available on the structure of the industry and a lack of consistency in reporting of international trade and market survey data on recycled plastics. This limits evidence-based strategic decisions and intervention, prevents existing actors from entering new markets and discourages new market entrants.

6.1.2. Technical barriers

There are numerous technical barriers associated with producing high quality, high value recycled plastics:

1. **Collection systems for wastes (including plastics) are not available for a substantial proportion of the global population.** An estimated 2 billion people globally do not have access to basic waste collection services, meaning that large quantities of waste plastics are not collected at all in lower income countries, particularly in rapidly developing, unplanned urban areas. Plastics which are collected are done so informally. Furthermore, a significant proportion of plastics waste escapes from the formal waste management system into the wider environment and is burnt or dumped, often ending up in rivers or marine environments where it becomes very difficult to recover.

2. **Plastics contaminated and mixed with other materials.** This is associated with several interrelated issues:

   a. Contamination levels in post-consumer plastics are often very high, necessitating removal using appropriate equipment. Whilst there are some technologies which have the potential to be used for recycling contaminated plastics, they have not yet been demonstrated to be commercially viable for recycling post-consumer plastics waste.

   b. Identifying and successfully separating polymers that are mixed together in the waste stream is technically challenging, particularly for certain polymers and materials (e.g. coloured black PP is difficult to separate from other types of plastics because it is not readily identified by automatic sorting equipment).

   c. Different polymers that are combined within products, in the form of mixed-material components or assemblies of components, presents challenges in disassembly and separation to extract target polymers (e.g. plastics used in multi-layer laminated packaging materials and plastics used in waste electrical and electronic equipment).

   d. The large number of different types of polymer and additives used increases the challenge.

3. **Problematic additives**. Some additives used in primary plastics can have a detrimental effect on the physical characteristics of recycled plastics (for example, affecting brittleness, flame retardancy, oxidation). A critical issue is that of degradability enhancers which can significantly affect the strength and durability of recycled plastics and, if they were to become widespread in primary plastics could potentially prevent plastics recycling entirely. Furthermore, the uncertainty around the presence and nature of additives that may be present in primary plastics can dis-incentivise plastics recycling because recyclers cannot be certain that their feedstocks are free from additives.
4. **Biodegradable plastics mixing with other plastics**. Biodegradable plastics are not suitable for recycling using conventional mechanical recycling techniques. Some biodegradable plastics exhibit the same characteristics as non-biodegradable materials (e.g. PLA and PET). This can lead to misclassification when materials are discarded, contaminating both recyclate streams and biological treatment facilities alike.
5. **Limited collection schemes and treatment technologies for thermosets**. Collection systems for thermosets are not well-established and are thought to be limited to commercial and industrial sources, and some specific items that arise in the municipal waste (e.g. household appliances). Technologies for recycling thermosets are also limited.

6.1.3. Environmental barriers

There are three key environmental barriers associated with recycling plastics:

1. **Hazardous additives**. Hazardous additives used in primary plastics can make their way into recycled plastics where they may pose a health risk, particularly where they are present in products that are used for sensitive applications such as toys and food packaging. This concern is compounded by the lack of transparency in the use of additives in plastics. This is a key issue for food contact plastics, which must be sourced from non-hazardous plastics waste.
2. **Competition between recycling and energy from waste**. There is a risk that, in specific contexts, energy-from-waste will compete for access to waste plastics as a feedstock thus pushing plastics towards a less-preferred option in environmental terms.
3. **Concerns about relatively weak environmental standards** may lead to restrictions on the flow of plastics waste (and derivatives) to jurisdictions where recycling costs are the lowest

6.1.4. Regulatory barriers

The regulatory barriers identified are:

1. **Regulatory burden of materials classified as waste**. Regulatory requirements that affect materials classified as a "waste" can create additional costs for recyclers and also reduce the perceived value of recycled material.
2. **Illegal trafficking in waste plastics**. A large proportion of waste plastics are traded illegally. The illegal waste trade is estimated at USD 10-12 billion annually (ISWA, 2014[69]). This has a significant effect on plastics trade as it undermines the quality of compliant material.
3. **Uncontrolled dumping and burning of wastes**. Poor enforcement against illegal disposal of wastes can undermine the market for recycled plastics.

6.2. Potential interventions

6.2.1. Identification of interventions

Given the diversity and scale of the challenge that markets for recycled plastics face, a range of measures and interventions will be needed. This will require close partnership amongst all stakeholders, including policy-makers, regulators, municipalities, industry and communities.

Five main categories of policy interventions plastics are considered here (following Taylor et al. 2012[68]):

1. **Regulatory** (e.g. banning plastics from landfill or setting statutory targets for recycling).
2. **Economic instruments** (e.g. a virgin resource tax)
3. **Technology** (e.g. development of new technologies for recycling mixed plastics).
4. **Data and information** (e.g. better market data or sharing of best practice)
5. **Voluntary measures** (e.g. an industry-led initiative towards single polymer use in packaging systems or better labelling and declarations on plastic packaging).

Each of the barriers identified in the study has been considered in terms of the potential interventions that could be used to address the barrier (see Table 6.1). Some potential interventions have not been included as they are considered too impractical or controversial.

The questionnaire responses provided by respondent countries gives some information on different policies implemented in different countries. The data provided by different responses was very variable in the level of detail and scope but, where possible, the information provided was used to inform the intervention mapping process presented below. For information, an overview of the policy information provided in the OECD questionnaires can be found in Annex P.

Table 6.1. **Mapping of barriers and potential interventions for recycled plastics**

No.	Barrier	Intervention				
		Regulatory	Economic instrument	Technology	Data and information	Voluntary
Economic barriers						
1	**Costs of collecting, sorting and processing waste plastics.**	Drive supply of recycled material to increase economies of scale and reduce costs by: • Setting targets for recycling. • Banning plastics from landfill. • Implementing extended producer responsibility regulation. • Standardising waste collection systems.	• Invest in collection infrastructure to reduce operating costs (e.g. collection vehicles, shredders and balers to reduce recycling transport costs). • Charge waste producers for collection and disposal of non-recyclable waste.	• Support development of more cost-effective technologies for sorting waste plastics. • Develop alternative technologies that enable recyclers to process poor quality material (e.g. low value and contaminated materials).	• Raise public awareness to create demand for plastics recycling, reduce contamination, and to reduce littering and dumping. • Share best practice on all aspects of the collection, sorting and reprocessing supply chain.	• Create voluntary standards for collection, sorting and reprocessing.

Table 6.1. **Mapping of barriers and potential interventions for recycled plastics** *(continued)*

No.	Barrier	Intervention				
		Regulatory	Economic instrument	Technology	Data and information	Voluntary
2	**Limited resilience of the sector to market shocks.**	Drive supply to increase economies of scale and resilience by: • Setting targets for recycling • Banning plastics from landfill • Implementing extended producer responsibility regulation • Standardising waste collection systems.	• Use financial market mechanisms to increase the resilience of the market to fluctuations in prices (e.g. futures markets or centrally managed risk funds).		• Improve access to data on quality, price and quantity of materials available to reduce uncertainty for investors and potential market entrants.	
3	**Global markets concentrated in a small number of countries**	• Implement quality standards in order to re-open trade	• Support development of domestic reprocessing capacity to reduce reliance on global markets.		• Develop and share market information to allow actors to expand into new markets. A more globalised market will reduce reliance on a single actor.	
4	**Lack of differentiated demand for recycled plastics.**	• Mandate requirement for recycled content to create demand • Use public procurement policies to create demand for recycled content. • Obligate monomer manufacturers to buy back recycled plastics.	• Use taxes or trading mechanisms to internalise the externalities associated with primary plastics. This will support the price of recycled plastics. • Introduce tax incentives to encourage use of recycled plastics.		• Provide information and training to designers and manufacturers to encourage use of recycled content. • Provide information to consumers to encourage purchase of products using recycled content and drive demand.	• Work with supply chain to encourage use of recycled content.
5	**Poor data on the plastics recycling industry.**	• Introduce mandatory data reporting mechanisms for plastics recycling.			• Develop and share appropriate data sources to stimulate the market and encourage new entrants, including standardising terminology and developing market-enabling tools and services.	
Technical barriers						
1	**Collection systems for wastes not available for a substantial proportion of the global population.**		• Mobilise investment for developing collection systems in low income contexts and incorporate plastics. Note: in these contexts, working with the informal sector will be essential.	• Development of appropriate low-tech plastics reprocessing technology that is suitable for use in low-income economies.	• Share best practice on all aspects of waste collection, sorting and recycling. • Raise consumer awareness to create demand for plastics recycling, reduce contamination, and to reduce littering and dumping.	

Table 6.1. **Mapping of barriers and potential interventions for recycled plastics** *(continued)*

No.	Barrier	Intervention: Regulatory	Economic instrument	Technology	Data and information	Voluntary
2	**Plastics contaminated and mixed with other materials**	• Standardise recycling collection schemes to create economies of scale and improve recyclate quality.		• Support technology innovation for sorting plastics and removing contamination or handling contaminated plastics. • Support the development and demonstration of alternative technologies for mixed and/or low value plastics.	• Share best practice on recycling collection schemes, sorting processes and recycling technologies. • Raise consumer awareness to create demand for plastics recycling, reduce contamination, and to reduce littering and dumping.	• Industry-led initiative to standardise polymers and additives.
3	**Problematic additives.**	• Ban or reduce these additives in primary plastics.	• Tax additives that cause detrimental effects on recycled plastics. • Tax degradability enhancers to disincentives their use.	• Develop alternatives to problematic additives. • Develop technologies that can identify these additives so that they can be eliminated from recycled plastics. • Develop purifying and stabilising technologies that can overcome the physical effects of these additives in recycled plastics.	• Enhance supply chain awareness of problematic additives so that the impact on markets for recycled plastics is understood.	• Industry-led phase out of problematic additives from primary plastics. • Standardise the use of additives and improve the information provided.
4	**Biodegradable plastics mixing with other plastics.**	• Mandate labelling for biodegradable plastics and improve associated standards		• Develop technologies for identifying biodegradable plastics. • Develop purifying and stabilising technologies that can overcome the physical effects of biodegradable plastics in waste plastics streams.	• Provide clear labelling and information for biodegradable plastics to encourage appropriate management by consumers.	
5	**Limited collection schemes and treatment technologies for thermosets.**	• Set targets (including using EPR) for recycling thermosets to drive supply.		• Develop and demonstrate effective collection and recycling systems for thermosets.	• Raise consumer awareness to create demand for recycling schemes for thermosets.	

Table 6.1. **Mapping of barriers and potential interventions for recycled plastics** *(continued)*

No.	Barrier	Intervention: Regulatory	Intervention: Economic instrument	Intervention: Technology	Intervention: Data and information	Intervention: Voluntary
Environmental barriers						
1	**Hazardous additives.**	• Ban or reduce hazardous additives from primary plastics.		• Develop alternatives to hazardous additives. • Develop technologies for identifying or tracking hazardous additives so that they can be eliminated from recycled plastics.	• Reduce uncertainty over the health effects of hazardous additives.	• Industry-led phase out of hazardous additives from primary plastics.
2	**Competition between recycling and energy from waste.**	• Ban plastics from energy from waste.	• Incentivise recycling over energy from waste by introducing a tax to reflect the relative environmental burden/benefit of energy from waste and recycling (and landfill).			
3	**Concerns over environmental standards for recycling in emerging markets.**	• Regulation and enforcement to ensure consistent environmental standards. • Mandate sellers to establish and audit end-destinations for environmental standards.			• Encourage openness about standards and provide information on end-destinations.	• Industry-led initiative to ensure consistent environmental standards in global markets.
Regulatory barriers						
1	**Regulatory burden of materials classified as waste.**	• Ensure regulation is proportionate and clarify end-of-waste standards.				• Develop effective voluntary standards for recycling sector to limit need for regulation.
2	**Uncontrolled dumping and burning of municipal wastes.**	• Enforcement action to reduce illegal dumping, particularly in low and middle income countries where uncontrolled dumping is still widespread.			• Raise public awareness to create demand for plastics recycling, reduce contamination, and to reduce littering and dumping.	
3	**Illegal trafficking in waste plastics.**	• Enforcement action.				• Industry-led initiatives to crack down on waste crime.

6.2.2. Assessment of potential interventions

An initial assessment of the interventions identified in Table 6.1 has been undertaken to consider their potential to improve markets for recycled plastics. This assessment is intended to provide a basis for understanding the types of interventions that have been, or could be, applied to support these markets.

Each intervention has been qualitatively assessed in terms of three factors:

- **Instrument maturity:** the extent to which the proposed intervention has been applied in the context of recycled plastics, or in similar recycled materials markets.
- **Instrument feasibility:** the feasibility of implementing the proposed intervention, particularly in terms of the extent to which different stakeholders would need to work together.
- **Instrument impact:** the potential impact of the proposed intervention in terms of the number and significance of barriers that it could potentially address.

The maturity, feasibility, and potential impact of each intervention has been evaluated qualitatively on the basis of the authors' expert opinion. Questionnaire responses were also used to provide a more quantitative insight into the policies that have already been implemented in respondent countries (i.e. instrument maturity). The potential impact of each intervention was assessed primarily on the impact it has had when implemented historically.

The interventions identified in Table 6.1 can be separated into four groups on the basis of the three factors identified above (see Annex Q for a detailed assessment of individual interventions, and Table 6.2 and Figure 6.1 for summary information):

- Interventions that are both mature and that have a demonstrated moderate to high impact
- Interventions that are less mature but that are potentially feasible and that could address a number of key barriers
- Interventions that are less mature and more challenging to implement (i.e. moderately feasible), but that could address a number of key barriers
- Other interventions that are either considered relatively infeasible or that have a limited impact.

The first three of these groups are considered to be the strongest potential interventions for addressing the barriers to the proper functioning of markets for recycled plastics. Each is discussed below.

Interventions that are well established and have a demonstrated impact:

- **Set statutory targets for recycling to drive supply of material, increase economies of scale, reduce costs and increase resilience.** The European Union's Waste Framework Directive set recycling targets to be achieved by EU Member States by 2020, including recycling rates of 50% by weight for household wastes and 70% for construction and demolition waste. These targets are thought to have been instrumental in driving up recycling rates in the EU. Statutory plastics recycling targets are considered to be essential to drive supply of waste plastics for recycling. It is important in this context to note that weight-based targets, as applied to-date in the EU for example, can skew activity away from plastics towards heavier materials.

There have been attempts to address the limitations of weight-based statutory targets by using metrics that reflect the different greenhouse gas emissions mitigation potential associated with recycling different materials (e.g. the Scottish carbon Metric).

- **Use Extended Producer Responsibility (EPR) regulation to drive supply of material and increase economies of scale, reduce costs and increase resilience.** EPR is well-established in Europe and a number of other countries. It has been successful in driving recycling for specific materials, including plastics. However, EPR has come under criticism from both the public and private sector for the ways in which the fees from producers are used to fund recycling systems. The implementation of successful EPR is complex, and warrants detailed assessment in its own right, but overall it is considered that these schemes have a key role to play in driving recycling. As with statutory targets, however, EPR generally has a limited impact on demand side.
- **Raise public awareness to create demand for plastics recycling, reduce contamination and to reduce dumping and uncontrolled dumping.** Raising consumer awareness of the issues surrounding waste plastics is critical to encouraging behaviours that support recycling and discourage littering and uncontrolled dumping and burning of wastes.

Interventions that are less well established, but that are potentially feasible, and that could have a significant impact:

- **Use public sector procurement policies to create demand for recycled content.** Due to the scale of its purchasing power, public sector procurement policies could create strong demand for recycled content. Many countries have introduced public procurement requirements to increase the purchase of recycled-content products (e.g. UK, Italy, France, Norway, the Netherlands, Spain, Belgium, Latvia, Japan, USA). This has the potential to increase economies of scale and demand for recycled content. Initial review indicates that there is limited clear evidence of success for driving demand for recycled plastics but it is thought that, it were if implemented widely and explicitly targeted plastics (among other materials), this could have a high impact.
- **Share best practice on all aspects of the collection, sorting and reprocessing supply chain.** Development of effective waste management systems that also include effective plastics collection, sorting and recycling elements is challenging. It requires appropriate technologies, sustainable financing and revenues, robust institutions and supportive consumer behaviour. A wide range of skills is needed to address these challenges but there are many successful examples. Sharing best practice on these issues will support the development of effective waste plastics collection, sorting and recycling industries.
- **Develop and share market information to allow actors to expand into new markets.** Data on the trade and movement of waste plastics is poor. Providing more robust data at a greater level of granularity would allow more informed decision to be made by existing actors in the sector and encourage new entrants to the market. It could help improve the efficiency of markets for recycled plastics and reduce reliance on a small number end-market destination for waste plastics. This data needs to be based on standardised definitions and also needs to include

market-enabling tools. One example efforts to provide better information and data on recycled materials is the Scottish Materials Brokerage Service (see Box 6.1).

- **Work with the supply chain to encourage use of recycled content** Efforts to encourage designers, manufacturers and major brands to use recycled content within their products will be essential for creating differentiated demand for recycled material. This approach has been particularly successful for encouraging the recycling of PET bottles for example by setting guidelines for designing for recyclability. The Plastics Industry Recycling Action Plan (PIRAP) is another example of a wider initiative. More recently, major brands such as Evian (Webster, 2018[70]) and Coca-Cola (The Guardian, 2017[71]) have committed to using recycled content in their packaging. This has the potential to create long-term demand for recycled content and encourage the recycled plastics supply chain to invest in new capacity.
- **Provide information and training to designers and manufacturers to encourage use of recycled content.** Creating demand for recycled plastics requires that all parts of the value chain are engaged and informed. Designers and manufacturers represent a key step in the chain. Small and medium sized enterprises (SME) are particularly important in this context as these organisations can rapidly develop new niches which can be scaled up as market demand grows. Without the engagement of designers and manufacturers, is unlikely that the incorporation of recycled content will become the norm for manufacturing new plastics products. Some countries (e.g. Belgium and the USA) have supported the development of tools for helping designers and producers compare the environmental impact of a primary raw material and a recycled variant. For example, the development of guidance for designing recyclable PET bottles by the European PET Bottle Platform (EPBP,(n.d.)[72]) and Recoup's recyclable packaging guidance has been key in rapidly increasing the proportion of PET bottles.
- **Provide information to consumers to encourage purchase of products using recycled content and drive demand.** Raising public awareness has the potential to encourage the public to use its purchasing power to encourage the supply chain to make products that are more recyclable and that use more recycled content. Consumer awareness has grown over recent decades but recyclability and recycled content is still not considered by most major brands to be a key factor in motivating consumer purchasing, although this situation is beginning to change (see commitments by Evian and Coca Cola cited above). Recycled content labels could be used to convey this type of information.

Box 6.1. Scottish Materials Brokerage Service

The Scottish government created The Scottish Materials Brokerage Service in 2014 to deal with the fragmented recycled materials market (see Annex F). The brokerage service helps match supply with demand for high-value recycled materials. The Brokerage aims to provide increased market stability for recycled materials; economies of scale by allowing local authorities in Scotland to pool materials; quality specifications built into contracts; and identify local opportunities for reprocessing materials (Zero Waste Scotland, 2017[73]).

Interventions that are less well established and that are more challenging to implement, but that could have a significant impact:

- **Enforcement action to reduce illegal dumping, particularly in low and middle income countries where dumping is commonplace.** Enforcement action is a key function of all regulatory systems. However, the degree to which it is effective depends upon the approach used and the level of resources available. Low income countries, in particular, often struggle to provide the resources necessary to implement effective enforcement for waste management. Notwithstanding these issues, regulatory approaches are essential for preventing illegal waste activity and are a prerequisite for properly functioning markets.
- **Enforcement action to reduce illegal waste trafficking.** International agreements (i.e. Basel Convention) provide the basis for regulating international waste movements. However, international co-operation and action is also essential to prevent illegal trafficking. As with local regulation (above), enforcement is a prerequisite for properly functioning markets.
- **Mandate requirement for recycled content to create demand.** No examples of mandatory requirements for recycled content have been identified during this study. Enforcing the requirement to include recycled content in products could stimulate demand for recycled content. However, it could also result in considerable cost to the industry if capacity is not in place to meet demand. This measure would require careful consideration.
- **Mobilise investment for developing collection, sorting and processing systems, particularly in low income contexts.** Returning waste plastics back into the manufacturing process requires capacity in collection systems and appropriate treatment, which is currently insufficient and, in some regions, is absent entirely. This will require investment. Generating the necessary capital finance and revenues to provide sustainable waste collection and sorting processes is very challenging. Clearly, this will require partnership between government sources of fund and commercial investment. Close partnership with the informal sector, which collects much of the recyclable plastics in low and middle income countries will also be essential. An example of an initiative that is underway to attempt to mobilise private finance to invest in the sector is the Closed Loop Fund (see Box 6.2).

Box 6.2. **Closed Loop Fund**

The Closed Loop Fund is managed by Closed Loop Partners which is a social investment group that raises finance for investment in sustainable consumer goods, advanced recycling technologies and the development of the circular economy. Until recently, the organisation focused on North America where it has raised USD 100 million from retailers and brand owners to help finance recycling operations. However, working in partnership with the Ocean Conservancy, Closed Loop Partners have recently announced development of a USD 150 million fund to support bankable recycling schemes in South East Asia, a region considered to be a key source of ocean plastics pollutions (Closed Loop Partners, 2017[73]).

- **Use financial market mechanisms to increase the resilience of the market to fluctuations in prices** (e.g. **futures markets or centrally managed risk funds).** The use of market-based financial instruments for managing risk in markets for recycled plastics appears to have had very limited application to-date. Two main approaches could, in theory be used: futures markets and centrally-managed risk funds. Neither appears to have been explored or implemented to any great extent, although the Chicago Board of Trade's Recyclables Exchange did operate a futures-based mechanism from 1995 to 1999. However, it was closed due to a range of problems including a lack of reliable specification and price transparency (Eunomia, 2015[74]). In principal these mechanisms have good potential to help the sector become more resilient to market shocks and warrant further consideration.

- **Support development of domestic reprocessing capacity to reduce reliance on global markets.** This will require action by national governments and industry. There has been some investment in Europe and North America around this issue but the activity has been largely focused on collection and sorting systems, rather than domestic recycling capacity.
- **Use taxes or trading mechanisms to internalise the externalities associated with primary plastics.** To-date a primary resource tax has not been implemented. Conceptually, this has the potential to make recycled plastics more competitively priced but its implementation could be very complex (e.g. what materials should be taxed and at what rates?) and it might be difficult to avoid unintended consequences particularly in terms of significant change to the primary plastics industry. Carbon markets are a related type of market mechanism that seek to internalise the greenhouse gas has impacts of different sectors, including the primary plastics sector. However, this mechanism has had limited impact in terms of supporting initiatives focused upon recycled plastics. The use of market mechanisms of this type to promote the use of recycled plastics requires further assessment.
- **Provide support to recycled plastics through direct or indirect government support**, such as lower VAT rate on recycled material. This would help to reduce the current cost advantage of virgin plastics and be justified to the extent that the feedstock for recycled material was already taxed when it was first put on the market.
- **Support development of better and more cost-effective technologies for collecting, transporting and sorting waste plastics.** Technology developments have played, and will continue to play, a key role in overcoming the barriers to recycling (for example, see Box 6.3). The Ellen MacArthur Foundation's (EMF) New Plastics Economy Initiative has identified a number of key technology breakthroughs that have the potential to bring about a step change in plastics recovery and recycling (see Annex R). Some of these are clearly very aspirational (innovations which EMF refers to as "moon-shot" innovations). Technology innovation is also needed for lower income settings to provide appropriate low-tech plastics reprocessing technology (e.g. comminution and compression equipment to enable participation in/access to global/regional markets).

Box 6.3. Research into black post-consumer polypropylene

WRAP (2015[34]) supported research into the challenging issue of recycling post-consumer black polypropylene, which normally cannot be detected by NIR equipment used in automated Material Recycling Facilities. This research effort has made considerable progress in helping to identify and demonstrate technologies (in this case the use of detectable colourants) that can overcome a specific technical barrier to recycling a key stream of waste plastics. The research forms part of the UK industry's Road-map to better recycling for Black Plastics, part of the industry-led Plastics Industry Recycling Action Plan (BPF, 2017[90]).

- **Support the development and demonstration of commercially viable technologies for reprocessing mixed and/or low value plastics.** Development of technologies for recovering value (either as base chemicals or fuel) could provide a treatment option for plastics that are currently hard to treat. Some commercial scale pyrolysis and gasification plants that could address this need have been constructed and others are reportedly under construction. These technologies have not yet entered mainstream application and are still considered to be fairly marginal, although it is relatively well-established, albeit at a small level, in Japan. Investment in innovation and development of existing technological configurations is required to build confidence in the industry. However, careful consideration must be given to the environmental suitability of these technologies for different types of plastics. There is a risk that these technologies could divert waste plastics from mechanical recycling to a less-preferred option in environmental terms. It is also important to note in this context that there are other, innovative technology developments that are focusing on developing new processes for recycling specific polymers in closed loops, for example: Polystyrene Loop (European Union,(n.d.)[75]) that has developed a new process for recycling polystyrene; and Ioniqa,(n.d.)[80] has developed a process using magnetic fluids as part of its PET separation and reprocessing technology.
- **Industry-led initiative to standardise polymers and additives, and improve information on additives.** Simplifying the use of polymers and additives should aid recycling of waste plastics by reducing the complexity in waste plastics. The New Plastics Economy Initiative's Global Plastics Protocol represents an example of a wide range of stakeholders working together to address the issue of packaging plastics (see Box 6.4).

Box 6.4. **The New Plastics Economy**

The Ellen MacArthur Foundation-led new Plastics Economy Programme (EMF, 2016[31]) is a three year programme that brings together stakeholders from the across the supply chain to "rethink and redesign the future of plastics", with a focus on packaging. The programme comprises five elements:

1. A dialogue mechanism that brings together stakeholders from all parts of the supply chain including consumer goods companies, retailers, plastic producers and packaging manufacturers, and municipalities and businesses involved in collection, sorting and reprocessing plastics.
2. A Global Plastics Protocol which seeks to establish a globally agreed approach to reducing the complexity of polymers, additives, products and after-use systems. This ambitious component of the programme includes efforts to: co-ordinate pilot studies and demonstration projects; facilitate globally agreed design standards for plastic packaging; define global labelling and material marketing standards; and aid convergence towards consistent waste plastics collection and sorting systems.
3. Research into "Innovation Moonshots" – new technologies that could radically improve the scope to recycle plastics (Annex Q), including: improving sorting technologies; developing environmentally-benign plastics; and commercialising depolymerisation technologies.

Box 6.4. **The New Plastics Economy** *(continued)*

4. Development of an improved evidence base to help guide good decisions on plastics use. Specific areas of research include: quantifying the socio-economic impact of ocean plastics; exploring the scale-up of GHG-based plastics; exploring the role of EfW; and assessing the economic impact of substances of concern.
5. Stakeholder engagement to share and communicate information on plastics

One very recent initiative under the programme was the Circular Design Challenge award: a USD 2 million grant for concepts that promote circular economy principles. Winners of the prize include a returnable coffee cup concept (CupClub) and seaweed-based packaging manufacture (Evoware).

- **Industry-led initiatives to crack down on waste crime.** Concerted and co-ordinated effort from industry, national governments and international agencies will be essential to reduce illegal waste trafficking and create robust markets for recycled materials. For example, the International Solid Waste Association initiated action to reduce illegal trafficking of waste in 2014 but current action on this issue is unclear.

Table 6.2. **Summary of intervention assessment**

No.	Intervention	Barriers that could be addressed	Maturity	Feasibility	Impact
Regulatory					
1	Set statutory targets for recycling to drive supply of material, increase economies of scale, reduce costs and increase resilience.	• Costs of collecting, sorting and processing waste plastics. • Limited resilience of the sector to market shocks.	H	H	H
2	Ban plastics from landfill to drive supply of material and increase economies of scale, reduce costs and increase resilience.	• Costs of collecting, sorting and processing waste plastics. • Limited resilience of the sector to market shocks.	H	M	M
3	Use Extended Producer Responsibility (EPR) regulation to drive supply of material and increase economies of scale, reduce costs and increase resilience.	• Costs of collecting, sorting and processing waste plastics. • Limited resilience of the sector to market shocks.	H	M	H
4	Standardise waste collection systems to increase economies of scale and reduce costs.	• Costs of collecting, sorting and processing waste plastics. • Plastics contaminated and mixed with other materials.	M	M	M
5	Mandate requirement for recycled content to create demand.	• Lack of differentiated demand for recycled plastics.	L	M	H
6	Use public sector procurement policies to create demand for recycled content.	• Lack of differentiated demand for recycled plastics.	M	H	M/H
7	Introduce mandatory data reporting mechanisms for plastics recycling.	• Poor data on the plastics recycling industry.	M	H	M
8	Ban or reduce problematic additives in primary plastics.	• Problematic additives.	L	M	M
9	Mandate labelling for biodegradable plastics and improve associated standards.	• Bio-degradable plastics mixing with other plastics.	L	M	M
10	Set targets (including using EPR) for recycling thermosets to drive supply.	• Limited collection schemes and treatment technologies for thermosets.	L	M	M
11	Ban or reduce hazardous additives from primary plastics.	• Hazardous additives.	M	M	M

Table 6.2. **Summary of intervention assessment** *(continued)*

No.	Intervention	Barriers that could be addressed	Maturity	Feasibility	Impact
12	Ban plastics from energy from waste.	• Competition between recycling and energy from waste.	L	L/M	M
13	Ensure regulation is proportionate and clarify end-of-waste requirements.	• Regulatory burdens of materials classified as waste.	M	M	M
14	Enforcement action to reduce illegal dumping, particularly in low and middle income countries where dumping is common place.	• Uncontrolled dumping and burning of municipal wastes.	M	M	H
15	Enforcement action to reduce illegal waste trafficking.	• Illegal trafficking in waste plastics.	M	M	H
16	Regulation and enforcement to ensure consistent environmental standards in global markets.	• Concerns over environmental standards for recycling in emerging markets.	M	M	M
17	Mandate sellers to establish and audit end-destinations for environmental standards.	• Concerns over environmental standards for recycling in emerging markets.	L	L	M
18	Obligate monomer manufacturers to buy back recycled plastics	• Lack of differentiated demand for recycled plastics	L	L	M/H
	Economic instruments				
19	Mobilise investment for developing collection, sorting and processing systems, particularly in low income contexts.	• Costs of collecting, sorting and processing waste plastics. • Collection systems for wastes not available for a substantial proportion of the global population.	M	M	H
20	Use financial market mechanisms to increase the resilience of the market to fluctuations in prices (e.g. futures markets).	• Limited resilience of the sector to market shocks.	L	M	H
21	Support development of domestic reprocessing capacity to reduce reliance on global markets.	• Global markets concentrated in a small number of countries	M	M/H	M/H
22	Use taxes or trading mechanisms to internalise the externalities associated with primary plastics. This will support the price of recycled plastics.	• Lack of differentiated demand for recycled plastics.	L	L/M	H
23	Direct or indirect government support for recycled plastics, e.g. through lower VAT rate	• Lack of differentiated demand for recycled plastics	L	L/M	H
24	Tax additives that cause detrimental effects on recycled plastics (including degradability enhancers).	• Problematic additives.	L	L	M
25	Incentivise recycling over energy from waste by introducing a tax to reflect the relative environmental burden/benefit.	• Competition between recycling and energy from waste.	L	M	L/M
26	Introduce tax incentives to encourage use of recycled plastics (e.g. VAT exemptions).	• Lack of differentiated demand for recycled plastics.	L	L/M	M
27	Charge waste producers for collection and disposal of non-recyclable waste.	• Costs of collecting, sorting and processing waste plastics.	M	M	M
	Technology				
28	Support development of better and more cost-effective technologies for collecting, transporting and sorting waste plastics.	• Costs of collecting, sorting and processing waste plastics.	M	M	H
29	Support the development and demonstration of commercially viable technologies for mixed and/ or low value plastics.	• Plastics contaminated and mixed with other materials.	L	M	H
30	Develop alternatives to problematic and hazardous additives.	• Problematic additives.	L	M	M
31	Develop technologies that can identify or track problematic and hazardous additives so that they can be eliminated from recycled plastics.	• Problematic additives.	L	M	M

Table 6.2. **Summary of intervention assessment** *(continued)*

No.	Intervention	Barriers that could be addressed	Maturity	Feasibility	Impact
32	Develop purifying and stabilising technologies that can overcome the physical effects of problematic additives in recycled plastics.	• Problematic additives.	L	M	M
33	Develop technologies for identifying biodegradable plastics	• Biodegradable plastics mixing with other plastics.	L/M	M	M
34	Develop purifying and stabilising technologies that can overcome the physical effects of biodegradable plastics in waste plastics streams.	• Biodegradable plastics mixing with other plastics.	L	L	L/M
35	Develop and demonstrate effective systems for collecting and recycling thermosets.	• Limited collection schemes and treatment technologies for thermosets.	L/M	M	M
	Data and information				
36	Raise public awareness in order to create demand for plastics recycling, reduce contamination, and to reduce littering and dumping.	• Costs of collecting, sorting and processing waste plastics. • Collection systems for wastes not available for a substantial proportion of the global population. • Plastics contaminated and mixed with other materials. • Limited collection schemes and treatment technologies for thermosets. Uncontrolled dumping and burning of municipal wastes.	M/H	H	H
37	Share best practice on all aspects of the collection, sorting and reprocessing supply chain.	• Costs of collecting, sorting and processing waste plastics. • Collection systems for wastes not available for a substantial proportion of the global population. • Plastics contaminated and mixed with other materials.	M	H	H
38	Develop and share market information to allow actors to expand into new markets. A more globalised market will reduce reliance on a single actor.	• Poor data on the plastics recycling industry • Global markets concentrated in a small number of countries • Limited resilience of the sector to market shocks.	L	H	M/H
39	Enhance supply chain awareness of problematic additives so that the impact on markets for recycled plastics is understood.	• Problematic additives.	L/M	M	M
40	Provide information and training to designers and manufacturers to encourage use of recycled content.	• Lack of differentiated demand for recycled plastics.	M	H	H
41	Provide information to consumers to encourage purchase of products using recycled content and drive demand.	• Lack of differentiated demand for recycled plastics.	M	H	M/H
42	Provide clear labelling and information for biodegradable plastics to encourage appropriate management by consumers.	• Biodegradable plastics mixing with other plastics.	M	H	M
43	Reduce uncertainty over the health effects of hazardous additives.	• Hazardous additives.	M	M	M
44	Encourage openness about standards and provide information on end-destinations.	• Concerns over environmental standards for recycling in emerging markets.	L/M	M	M
	Voluntary				
45	Create voluntary standards for collection, sorting and reprocessing.	• Costs of collecting, sorting and processing waste plastics.	M	M	M
46	Work with supply chain to encourage use of recycled content.	• Lack of differentiated demand for recycled plastics.	M	H	H
47	Industry-led initiative to standardise polymers and additives, and improve information on additives.	• Separating polymers from other materials, other polymers and contamination.	M	M	M/H
48	Industry-led phase out of problematic and hazardous additives from primary plastics.	• Problematic additives.	M	M	M

Table 6.2. **Summary of intervention assessment** *(continued)*

No.	Intervention	Barriers that could be addressed	Maturity	Feasibility	Impact
49	Develop effective voluntary standards for recycling sector to limit need for regulation.	• Regulatory burdens of materials classified as waste.	L	M	M
50	Industry-led initiatives to crack down on waste crime.	• Illegal trafficking in waste plastics.	L/M	M	H
51	Industry-led initiative to ensure consistent environmental standards in global markets.	• Concerns over environmental standards for recycling in emerging markets.	L	L	M

Key: **H** High
M Medium
L Low

Figure 6.1. **Intervention mapping**

Notes: Please refer to Table 6.2 for details of each intervention (e.g. number 1 is the regulatory intervention "Set statutory targets", etc). Maturity, feasibility and potential impact have been assessed qualitatively and allocated to one of the areas in the diagram. Relative positions within each area are not intended to represent relative feasibility and impact. Please refer to text for further details.

References

BPF (2017), *Plastics Industry Recycling Action Plan*, www.bpf.co.uk/topics/pirap.aspx (accessed on 26 March 2018). [101]

Closed Loop Partners (2017), *CL Fund*, www.closedlooppartners.com/closed-loop-fund/ (accessed on 26 March 2018). [100]

EMF (2016), "The New Plastics Economy", https://www.ellenmacarthurfoundation.org/assets/downloads/EllenMacArthurFoundation_TheNewPlasticsEconomy_15-3-16.pdf (accessed on 26 March 2018). [34]

EPBP (n.d.), *European PET Bottle Platform: Design Guidelines*, www.epbp.org/design-guidelines (accessed on 26 March 2018). [72]

Eunomia (2015), *Managing the Risk from Secondary Raw Material Price Movements*, www.eunomia.co.uk/reports-tools/managing-the-risk-from-secondary-raw-material-price-movements/ (accessed on 26 March 2018). [74]

European Union((n.d.)), *PolyStyreneLoop Project*, https://circulareconomy.europa.eu/platform/en/good-practices/polystyreneloop-project-pioneer-demonstration-plant-treat-3300-tonnes-polystyrene-wasteyr-2018 (accessed on 26 March 2018). [75]

Ioniqa (n.d.), *Ioniqa Technologies*, www.ioniqa.com/(accessed on 26 March 2018). [102]

ISWA (2014), "Global recycling markets: plastic waste", https://www.iswa.org/fileadmin/galleries/Task_Forces/TFGWM_Report_GRM_Plastic_China_LR.pdf (accessed on 26 March 2018). [33]

Taylor, C. et al. (2012), "Selecting Policy Instruments for Better Environmental Regulation: a Critique and Future Research Agenda", *Environmental Policy and Governance*, Vol. 22/4, pp. 268-292, http://dx.doi.org/10.1002/eet.1584. [107]

The Guardian (2017), *Coca-Cola to increase amount of recycled plastic in its bottles* |, https://www.theguardian.com/business/2017/jul/11/coca-cola-to-radically-increase-amount-of-recycled-plastic-in-its-bottles (accessed on 26 March 2018). [71]

Webster, B. (2018), *Evian to switch to 100% recycled plastic bottles by 2025*, The Times, https://www.thetimes.co.uk/article/evian-promises-move-to-purely-recycled-bottles-by-2025-sclfm8cqz (accessed on 26 March 2018). [70]

WRAP (2017), *Materials Pricing Report*, www.wrap.org.uk/content/materials-pricing-report (accessed on 26 March 2018). [9]

Zero Waste Scotland (2017), *Scottish Materials Brokerage Service*, www.zerowastescotland.org.uk/brokerage (accessed on 26 March 2018). [73]

Annex A

Overview of plastics production processes

Figure A.1. **Manufacturing plastics from raw material**

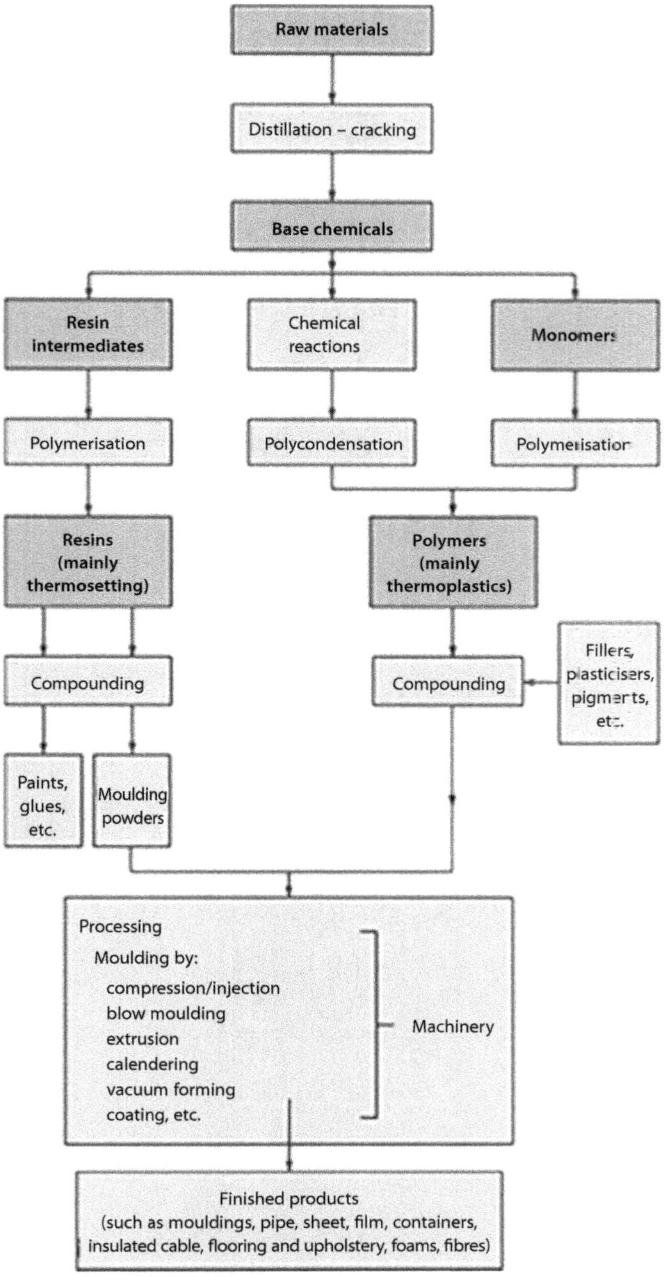

Source: International Labour Office (2012[24]), *Chemical Industry*, http://bit.ly/2ywVOQJ.

Figure A.2. **PET recycling process**

PET: Polyethylene Terephthalate
A-PET: Amorphous PET
R-PET: Reclaimed PET
SSP: Solid-state Polymerisation
PET-SSR: PET Solid State Resin

ISBM: Injection Stretch Blow Moulding
ER: Engineering Resin
PC: Post-Consumer
PI: Post-Industry
MSW: Municipal Solid Waste

trade
Stock
Process

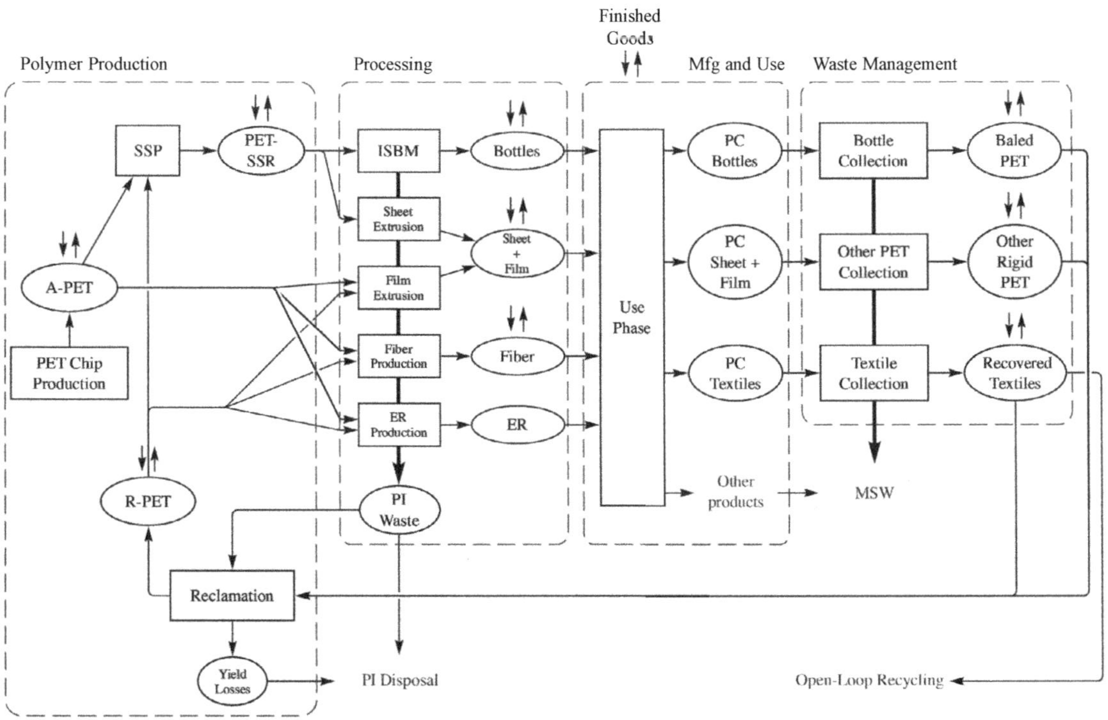

Source: COWI (2013[15]), *Hazardous substances in plastics materials*, http://bit.ly/2td8BY2.

Annex B

Additives

Table B.1. **Summary of additives used in plastics**

Type of additive	Typical amount in % w/w	Comments	Substances
Functional additives			
Plasticisers	10-70	Around 80 % used in PVC and the remaining 20 % in cellulose plastic	Short and medium chain chlorinated paraffins (SCCP-MCCP); Diisoheptylphthalat (DIHP); DHNUP; Benzyl butyl phthalate (BBP); Bis (2-ethylhexyl)phthalate (DEHP): Bis(2-methoxyethyl) phthalate (DMEP): Dibutyl phthalate (DBP); Diisobutyl phthalate (DiBP); Tris(2-chloroethyl)phosphate (TCEP);
Flame retardants	12-18 (for brominated)	Three groups: organic non-reactive, reactive; inorganics.	Short and medium chain chlorinated paraffins (SCCP-MCCP): Boric acid; Brominated flame retardants: Tris(2-chloroethyl)phosphate (TCEP)
Stabilisers, Antioxidants and UV stabilizers Heat stabilisers	0.05-3 0.5-3	Amount depends on chemical structure of additive and of plastic polymer. Phenolic antioxidants are used in low amounts and phosphites in high. Lowest amounts in polyolefins (LLDPE, HDPE), higher in HIPS and ABS Used in PVC. Based on lead, tin, barium, cadmium and zinc compounds. Lead is most efficient and used in the lower amounts.	Bisphenol A (BPA); Cadmium compounds; Lead compounds; Nonylphenol compounds; Octylphenol; 1,3,5-Tris(oxiran-2-ylmethyl)-1,3,5-triazinane-2,4,6-trione (TGIC)/1,3,5-tris[(2S and 2R)2,3-epoxypropyl]-1,3,5triazine-2,4,6-(1H,3H,5H)trione (TGIC) Cadmium compounds; Lead compounds; Nonylphenol (barium and calcium salts);
Slip agents	0.1-3	Amounts depend on chemical structure of slip agent and plastic polymer type	
Lubricants (internal and external)	0.1-3		
Antistatics	0.1-1	Most types are hydrophilic and can migrate to water	
Curing agents	0.1-2	Peroxides and other crosslinkers, catalysts, accelerators	4,4'-Diaminodiphenylmethane (MDA); 2,2'-dichloro-4,4'-methylenedianiline (MOCA); Formaldehyde – reaction products with aniline; Hydrazine; 1,3,5-Tris(oxiran-2-ylmethyl)-1,3,5-triazinane-2,4,6-trione (TGIC)/1,3,5-tris[(2S and 2R)2,3-epoxypropyl]-1,3,5triazine-2,4,6-(1H,3H,5H)trione (TGIC)

Table B.1. **Summary of additives used in plastics** *(continued)*

Type of additive	Typical amount in % w/w	Comments	Substances
Blowing agents	Depends on the density of the foam and the potential gas production of the agent	Azodicarbonamide, benzene di-sulphonyl hydrazide (BSH), pentane, CO_2	
Biocides	0.001-1	Soft PVC and foamed polyurethanes are the major consumers of biocides. They are of different chemical structures and include chlorinated nitrogensulphur heterocycles and compounds based on tin, mercury, arsenic, copper and antimony, e.g. tributyltin and 10,10′-oxybisphenoarsine	Arsenic compounds; Organic tin compounds; Triclosan;
Colourants			
Soluble (eg. azocolorants)	0.25-5	Migrates easily. Used in highly transparent plastics. They are expensive, have limited light and heat resistance. They are used in PS, PMMA and cellulose plastics to give a bright transparent colour.	
Organic pigments	0.001-2.5	Insoluble low migration tendency	Cobalt(II) diacetate
Inorganic pigments	0.01-10	E.g. zinc sulphide, zinc oxide, iron oxide, cadmium-mangane based, chromium based, ultramarine and titanium dioxide	Camium compounds; Chromium compounds; Lead compounds
Special effect	Varies with the effect and substance in question	Aluminium and copper powder, lead carbonate or bismuthoxichloride and substances with fluorescence Substances with fluorescence might migrate, the former not	
Fillers	Up to 50	Calcium carbonate, talk,clay, zinc oxide, glimmer, metal powder, wood powder, asbest, barium sulphate, glass microspheres, silicious earth	
Reinforcements	Glass (15-30%)	Glass fibers, carbon fibers, aramide fibers. 15-30% is for glass only due to the high density of glass.	

Source: COWI (2013[14]), *Hazardous substances in plastics materials*, http://bit.ly/2td8BY2.

Plasticisers

Plasticisers make materials more flexible. In plastics production, plasticisers consist of small molecules that can dissolve into the liquid polymer (high miscibility) increasing its plasticity or viscosity. They may be solids or liquids. In plastics production there are over 300 types of plasticiser of which between 50 and 100 are in commercial use. Estimates for global production vary from 7.2 Mtpa (Geyer, Jambeck and Law, 2017[1])to 8 Mtpa (C&EN, 2015[76]); the largest group being phthalate esters which make up approximately 70% of global use (Figure B.1.).

Figure B.1. **Global plasticiser production 2014**

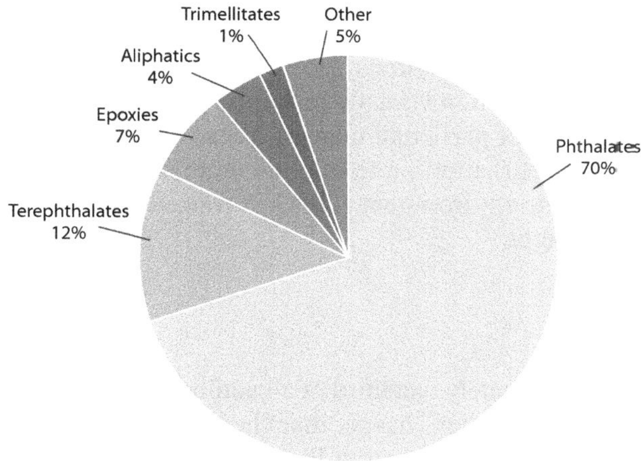

Source: IHS (2015), *Plasticizers*, https://ihsmarkit.com/products/plasticizers-chemical-economics-handbook.html.

Figure B.2. **Plasticiser production by region**

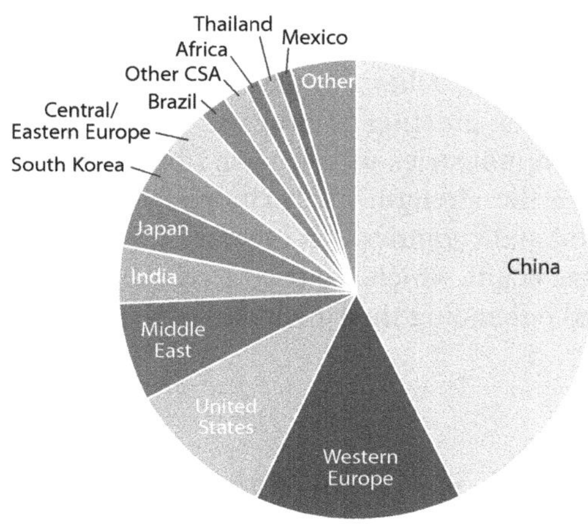

Source: IHS (2015), *Plasticizers*, https://ihsmarkit.com/products/plasticizers-chemical-economics-handbook.html.

Phthalates are used mainly in the production of PVC where they often comprise up to 30% of the final product but sometimes up to 50%. Around 80-90% of plasticisers are used in PVC manufacturing (IHS, 2015[77]). There are around 25 phthalates in existence (Halden, 2010[78]); the two most commonly used in industry are:

- di(2-ethylhexyl) phthalate (DEHP) also known as dioctyl phthalate
- diisononyl phthalate (DINP).

Although they have been used in plastics production since the 1940s, phthalates have been implicated in numerous health problems such as cancer. In particular, it has been demonstrated that phthalates can migrate out of plastic products and be absorbed into the body through:

- ingestion of contaminated materials such as contaminated food or house dust
- dermal uptake of phthalates from personal care products
- inhalation of air containing phthalates from off-gassing paints; wall, ceiling and floor coverings.

DEHP is classed by the US department of health as a product that is "reasonably anticipated to be a human carcinogen" and is the most common phthalate used, at approximately 2 Mtp (Vinyl Plus, 2014[79]). This is reducing as has been banned in the US in baby products since the early noughties. However, the drop in US production has been replaced by increased production in China which now produces approximately 40% of the world's plasticisers. DEHP is of particular concern because its low molecular weight (which also makes it a good plasticiser) allows it to migrate more readily from its host polymer and potentially into people or the environment. This has caused increasing use of DINP which has a higher molecular weight.

Fillers

"Fillers" make up approximately one third of all additives used in polymer processing and are used partly because they are often cheaper than the host polymer, but mainly because they improve the properties of the resin (Phantom Plastics,(n.d.)[80]). Fillers are almost entirely of mineral origin. Calcium carbonate is the most common, as it is inexpensive, soft and readily available in most geographies. It improves stiffness, strength and impact resistance. Other "inert" fillers include talc, kaolinite, wollastonite, and muscovite mica. These types of fillers have been entirely responsible for the ability of plastics like PP to compete in the engineering polymer market

One of the most well-known fillers is glass fibre which is used to reinforce both thermoplastics and thermosets; creating "fibreglass". This is particularly the case in the automotive and construction industries where glass fibres (and increasingly carbon fibres) are being used to improve the strength of thermoplastics to create composites that can compete with metals, wood and ceramics. An increasingly common companion additive to fibreglass products is glass beads which are used to reduce warpage as well as promoting flow during moulding and enhancing the finish of surfaces.

Flame retardants

Flame retardants have received a lot of negative publicity since the 1970s due to their persistence in the natural environment and human toxicity. However, the group of additives comprises around 175 products (Segev, Kushmaro and Brenner, 2009[81]) with diverse compositions.

The purpose of flame retardants is to slow combustion and allow greater escape time, reduce toxic gas release, smoke and heat. Predictably their main product use is in electrical and electronics (~53%), construction, and automotive furnishing sectors, in that order (Rutland Plastics,(n.d.)[82]).

Flame retardancy works via three broad mechanisms:

- **Vapour phase inhibition** is where additives react with the burning polymer as it vaporises, scavenging free radicals that would otherwise assist branching out of the radical chain reaction in the flame
- **Solid phase char formation** is where the additive forms a barrier layer on the material's surface which slows pyrolysis by inhibiting polymers from entering the vapour phase
- **Quench and cool** additives consist largely of hydrated minerals which release water via endothermic reactivity during combustion, quenching the fire

The compounds themselves can be divided into two broad groups:

1. Halogenated (bromine, chlorine in organic compound form)
2. Non-halogenated (also low smoke and fume [LSF]):
   - Aluminium hydroxides (ATH)
   - Magnesium hydroxides
   - Antimony oxides
   - Organo-phosphorus compounds
   - Others: Nitrogen compounds (such as melamine), boric acid & borates, ammonium polyphosphate and expandable graphite

(Anderson, 2015[83])

Market data varies on the amounts of flame retardants used. For instance, Geyer, Jambeck and Law (2017[1]) estimate total global consumption at approximately 2.7 Mtpa, Segev, Kushmaro and Brenner (2009[29]) estimate 1.5 Mtpa, Anderson (2015[31]) (2.24) and Ceresana (2016[32]) estimates 2.15 Mtpa.

Aluminium trihydrate (ATH) uses the "quench and cool" mechanism and is the most commonly used flame retardant globally accounting for 34% of all flame retardants.

Figure B.3. **Proportions of flame retardants used globally**

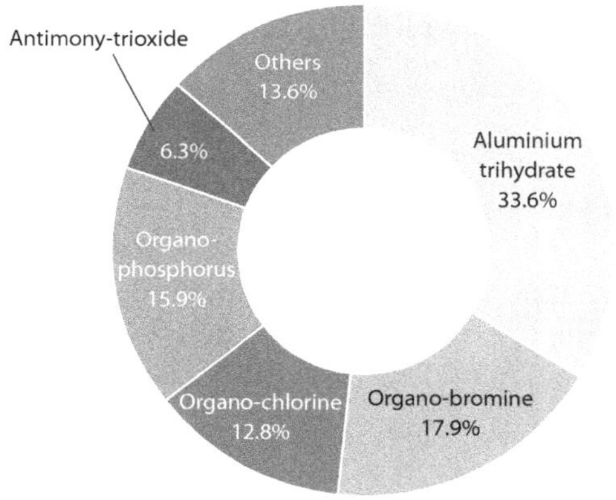

Source: Anderson (2015[31]), *ATH use in flame retardants: An overview of the industry and growth in Asia*, http://bit.ly/2gbds6h.

According to Roskill, organo-brominated flame retardants make up 18% of the market, accounting for 0.4 Mt of material produced each year. Estimates by Birnbaum and Staskal (2004[32]) reported production at 0.2 Mtpa indicting that it has doubled in the last 10 years. Other authors report brominated compounds to be the most widely used flame retardant, but this seems unlikely.

Bromine is particularly prized in flame retardants as it has a greater atomic weight and hence the compounds thermally decompose more slowly. Brominated flame retardants have been found throughout the food chain, in human tissue, breast milk and blood serum of exposed populations (recycling, production of plastics etc).

Harmful health effects observed as a consequence of brominated compound exposure include endocrine disruption, neurotoxicity, cytotoxicity, neurotoxicity, genotoxicity, immunotoxicity, mutagenicity, carcinogenicity and teratogenicity.

Bisphenol A (BPA)

BPA has been used since the 1950s as a hardener in the production of plastics such as epoxy resins and notably, polycarbonate which is often used for producing baby bottles. In polycarbonate, BPA is used as a base monomer in production, whereas it is considered an additive when used in other plastics such as PVC (Thompson et al., 2009[84]). Other uses include compact discs, impact-resistant safety equipment, and medical devices. BPA is used to harden epoxy resin lining which cover the internal surfaces of most metallic food and beverage containers.

BPA has received a huge amount of attention because of its potential as an endocrine disruptor and is found in 90% of humans in Europe and North America. Although no clear agreement exists on the amount of BPA which humans may be exposed to from food packaging (the most likely source-pathway), the USFDA (2014[33]) has banned the use of polycarbonate in baby bottles and infant formula packaging as a precaution. However, like the European Food Safety Authority (EFSA), the USFDA also concluded that there is no conclusive evidence to support a ban across the use of BPA in other applications.

BPA use is reported to be approximately 4.6 Mtpa and is growing by approximately 5% annually (Merchant Research & Consulting, 2013[85]). Content by mass varies considerably. For instance, PVC may contain 50-60% additives by mass, whereas PET bottles may contain just 1%; some examples of additive use in polymers are shown in Table 2.3.

Compatibilisers

Compatibilisers have long been used in the polymer industry to allow incompatible resins to be blended together; in particular to form new products with enhanced properties. Three broad groups exist: bipolar copolymer compatibilisers, maleated copolymer, and in-situ macromolecule catalysts. A more comprehensive list can be found in SPI: The Plastics Industry Trade Association (SPI, 2015[86]).

As well as achieving improved performance, compatibilisers can also assist recyclers with mixing heterogeneous materials, an issue common when handling post-consumer sources. This is pertinent for many reprocessors which often focus on one or two polymers but receive multiple types from sorters and collectors. Compatibilisers may provide a key to reducing rejected materials (reported to be approximately 15% for many US companies) and increasing profitability.

However, compatibilisers specifically target two or more types of resin but there is, as yet, no one-size-fits-all product on the market. Therefore their use is limited for highly heterogeneous blends and still requires compositional analysis to determine proportional content for adjusting the recipe.

Stabilisers

Cadmium/barium and lead have been used extensively in PVC production to improve heat resistance and weathering properties. The European Vinyl industry has agreed to eliminate both lead and cadmium/barium by 2001. However, although the use of lead has reduced, the industry has generally replaced it with cadmium/barium (Vinyl Plus, 2014[79]) (Figure B.4).

Figure B.4. **Use of lead and cadmium/barium stabilisers in the EU**

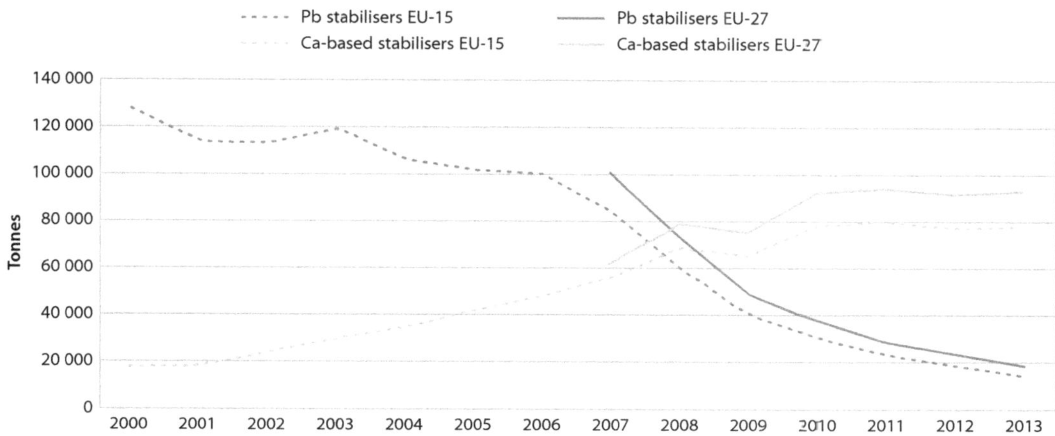

Source: Vinyl Plus (2014[27]), *The European PVC industry's experience in replacing lead and cadmium-based stabilisers*, http://bit.ly/2xyv66F.

China plans to phase out the use of lead but has not as yet made a commitment on cadmium/barium.

Historical use, mainly in construction, means that the majority of cadmium, barium and lead-containing PVC remains in stock, and will for many years arise in waste. The current approach used to address this issue in the EU is to restrict secondary use of these materials to construction, which have limited contact with humans and the environment (Villanueva and Eder, 2014[14]).

Degradability additives

Degradability additives are often added to conventional plastics to increase biodegradability or dispersion in the environment (ISRI, 2017[87]). Examples include biodegradable, oxo-degradable, and photo degradable additives. The extent to which these additives cause plastic to degrade is not supported by tests (ATSM or ISO for instance), therefore the fate of these materials in the environment is unclear.

Degradable additives do not necessarily lead to plastics becoming compostable and may not result in significant biodegradation at all. Rather, they may simply break the larger material mass into smaller fragments.

An unintended consequence of marketing plastics as biodegradable can result in materials being discarded as litter because consumers assume that they will break down naturally.

Biodegradable plastics almost certainly impede recycling as they inherently result in the material losing its strength and durability. Therefore uptake of these material across the plastics industry, although driven by well-meaning consumers, is slow.

Adhesives

Although adhesives are not an additive to plastics as such, their use can often impede recycling efforts as they cause incongruous objects to adhere to each other, which reduces the purity of target materials in sorting processes.

Additives to biodegradable plastics

An emerging concern identified by Moss et al. (2016) is that some biodegradable plastics may be modified with additives that would not migrate from a traditional resin. However, with a biodegradable host resin, the additives may release into the environment as it decomposes.

Annex C

Bioplastics

Bio-plastic typologies

Figure C.1. **Detailed typology of biopolymers**

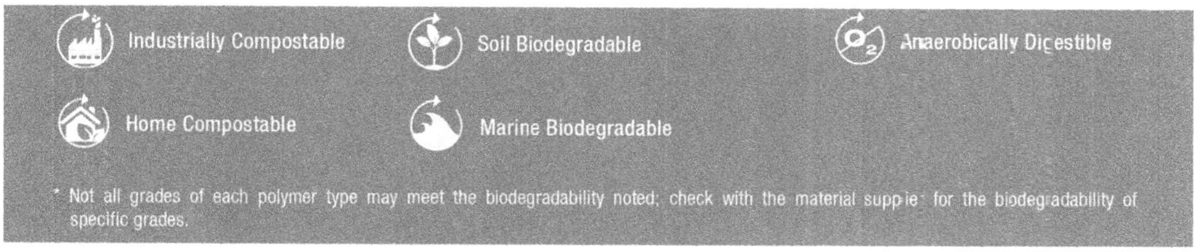

Polymer Abbreviation	Polymer Name	Biobased	Biodegradable
PHA	Polyhydroxy Alkanoate	Yes	
PLA	Polylactic Acid	Yes	
TPS	Thermoplastic Starch	Yes	
PBS	Polybutylene Succinate	Yes	
PBAT	Polybutylene Adipate-Co-Terephthalate	Partially	
PBAS	Polybutylene Adipate-Co-Succinate	In Development	
PES	Polyethylene Succinate	Partially And Fully Biobased In Development	No
PEF	Polyethylene Furanoate	In Development	No
PET	Polyethylene Terephthalate	Partially	No
PEET	Polyetherester Terephthalate	Partially	No
PTT	Polytrimethlene Terephthalate	Partially	No
PPA	Polyphthalamide	Partially	No
PA 410	Polyamide 410	Partially	No
PA 610	Polyamide 610	Partially	No
PA 1010	Polyamide 1010	Yes	No
PA 10	Polyamide 10	Partially	No
PA 11	Polyamide 11	Partially	No
TPC-ET	Thermoplastic Copolymer Elastomer	Partially	No
TPU	Thermoplastic Polyurethane	Partially	No
PE	Polyethylene	Yes	No
PP	Polypropylene	In Development	No

Source: Mashek (2016[88]), *Plastics Market Watch*, http://bit.ly/2xgEonQ.

Bioplastics production forecast by region

Figure C.2. **Bioplastics production in 2015 and forecasted production for 2020 by region**

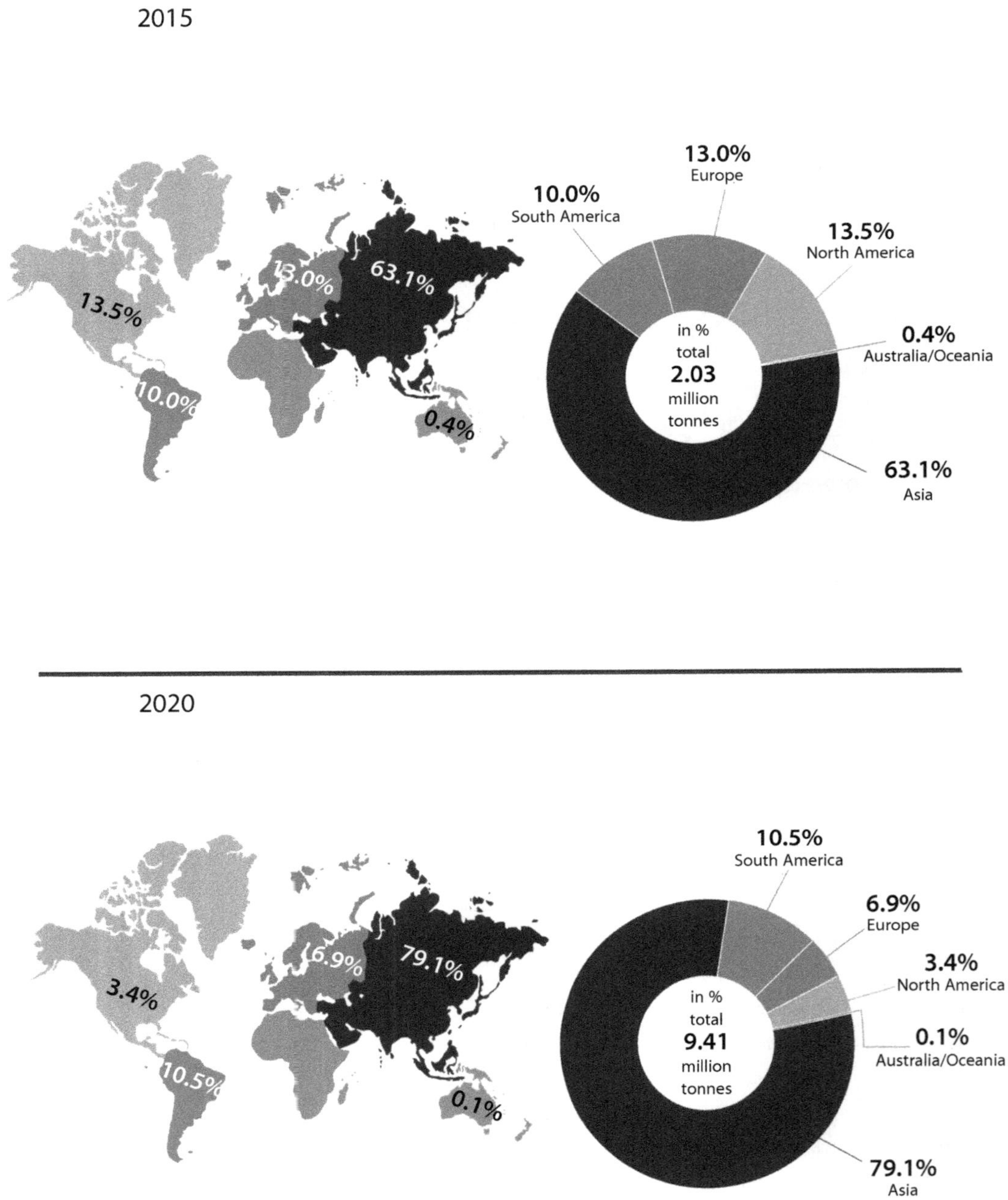

Source: Institute for Bioplastics and Biocomposites (2017[21]), *Biopolymers*, https://bit.ly/2HTeUmD.

Bioplastics forecast by polymer type

Figure C.3. **Global bioplastics production by polymer type in 2015**

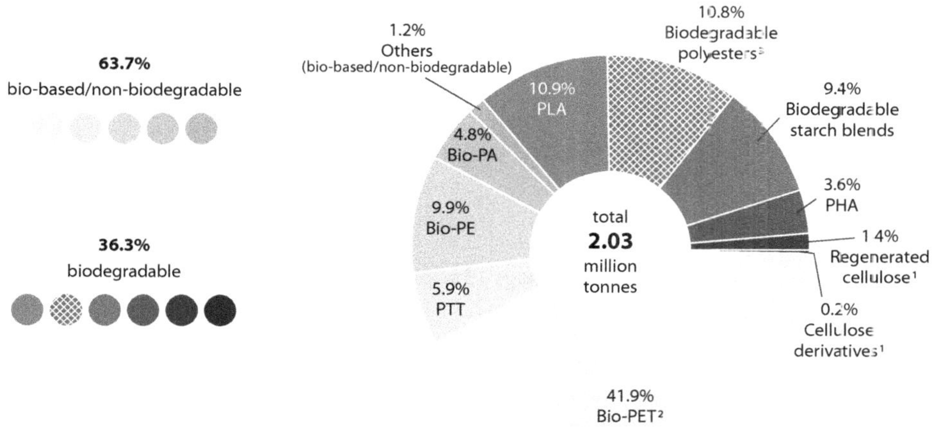

Notes: 1. Compostable hydrated cellulose fibres.
2. Bio-based contents amounts 30%.
3. Contains PBAT, PBS, PCL.

Source: Institute for Bioplastics and Biocomposites (2017[21]), *Biopolymers*, https://bit.ly/2HTeUmD.

Figure C.4. **Predicted global bioplastics production by polymer type in 2020**

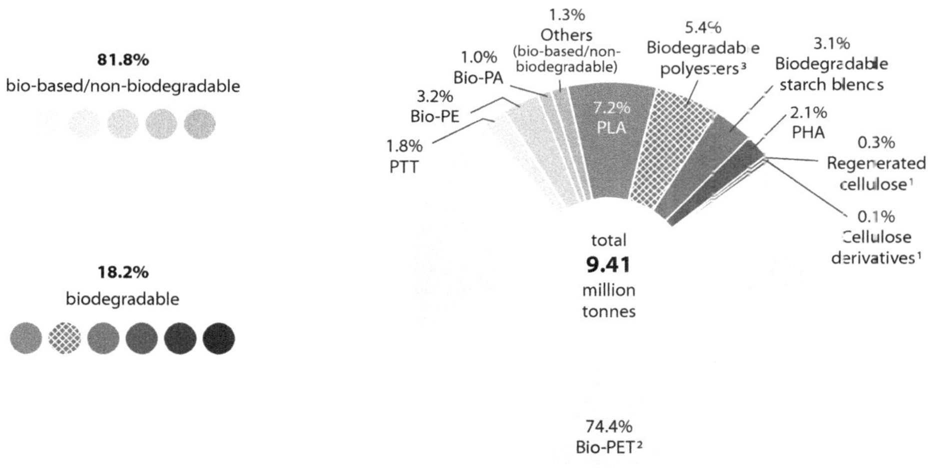

Notes: 1. Compostable hydrated cellulose fibres.
2. Bio-based contents amounts 30%.
3. Contains PBAT, PBS, PCL.

Source: Institute for Bioplastics and Biocomposites (2017[21]), *Biopolymers*, https://bit.ly/2HTeUmD.

Annex D

Degradation definitions

Table D.1. **Degradation definitions**

Term	Definition
Degradation	The partial or complete breakdown of a polymer as a result of e.g. UV radiation, oxygen attack, biological attack. This implies alteration of the properties, such as discolouration, surface cracking, and fragmentation.
Biodegradation	Biological process of organic matter, which is completely or partially converted to water, CO_2/ methane, energy and new biomass by microorganisms (bacteria and fungi).
Mineralisation	Defined here, in the context of polymer degradation, as the complete breakdown of a polymer as a result of the combined abiotic and microbial activity, into CO_2, water, methane, hydrogen, ammonia and other simple inorganic compounds.
Biodegradable	Capable of being biodegraded.
Compostable	Capable of being biodegraded at elevated temperatures in soil under specified conditions and time scales, usually only encountered in an industrial composter (standards apply).
Oxo-degradable	Containing a pro-oxidant that induces degradation under favourable conditions. Complete breakdown of the polymers and biodegradation still have to be proven.

Source: UNEP (2015[88]), *Biodegradable plastics and marine litter: misconceptions, concerns and impacts on marine environments*, http://bit.ly/2uEJLM8.

Annex E

Lifecycle analysis

System boundary for plastics

Figure E.1. **System flow and boundaries for plastics value chain**

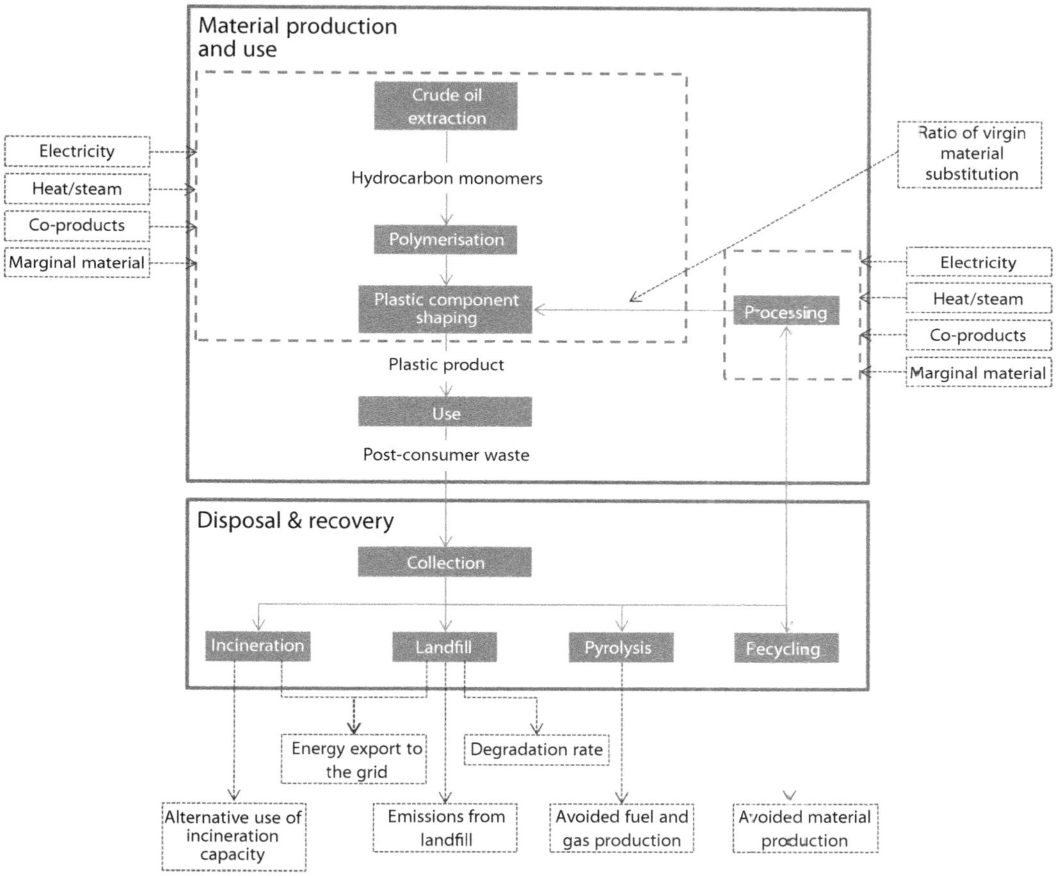

Source: Michaud, Farrant and Jan (2010[19]), *Environmental benefits of recycling*, http://bit.ly/2uricL6.

Lifecycle inventory data

Table E.1. **Carbon factors (kg CO_2/tonne savings versus landfill)**

Plastic type	kg CO_2/tonne saved by recycling compared to landfill
PET	1 705
PS	1 240
Mixed plastics	1 215
Mixed Plastic Bottles	1 156
HDPE	1 161
LDPE	1 098
PP	948
PVC	888
Other plastics	688

Note: ranked by highest impact from recycling.

Source: Defra (2012[84]), *England Carbon Metric*, http://bit.ly/2vm94o3

Table E.2. **Environmental inventories of PET production using virgin and recycled materials**

Input and output	1 kg virgin plastic (PET)	1 kg recycled plastic (R-PET)
Input		
Energy (& petroleum)	84 MJ	7.97 MJ
Waterborne	17.5 kg	2.96 kg
Other input materials	0.01 kg	0.024 kg
Output		
Atmospheric emission	6 kg	3.5 kg
Solid waste	45.13 kg	0.31 kg
Waterborne emission	21.46 kg	12.82 kg

Source: Wong (2009[88]), *A Study of Plastic recycling supply chain*, http://bit.ly/2vtHK7L.

Table E.3. **Relative difference between the impacts from the different end-of-life options vs. recycling for climate change for different plastic types**

	Recycling versus other alternatives										
No. case	1[PE]	1[PET]	2[MIX1]	2[MIX2]	2[MIX3]	2[MIX4]	3[PE]	3[PP]	3[PS]	3[PET]	3[PVC]
Incineration + energy rec.	310%	200%	390%	710%	390%	710%	990%	50%	100%	210%	0%
Landfill	100%	100%	130%	150%	130%	150%	1 080%	60%	130%	220%	10%
Pyrolysis			100%	110%	90%	80%					

	Recycling versus other alternatives										
No. case	4[MIX]	5[MIX]	6[HDPE]	6[LDPE]	6[PET]	7[PET]	7[PE]	7[PVC]	8[PS1]*	8[PS2]	8[PS3]
Incineration with energy rec.	430%	40%	170%	150%	170%				10%*	60%	100%
Landfill	290%		100%	100%	100%	130%	160%	110%			
Pyrolysis	30%										

*Feedstock recycling scenario.

Note: A positive value means that recycling is preferable to the other end-of-life option. A negative value means that recycling causes more environmental impact than the other end-of-life option.

Source: Michaud, Farrant and Jan (2010[19]), *Environmental benefits of recycling*, http://bit.ly/2uricL6.

Annex F

Scottish Carbon Metric Detail

Figure F.1. **Scottish Carbon Metric normalised to aluminium (100%) to show the relative reduction of CO2eq from recycling materials compared to landfill**

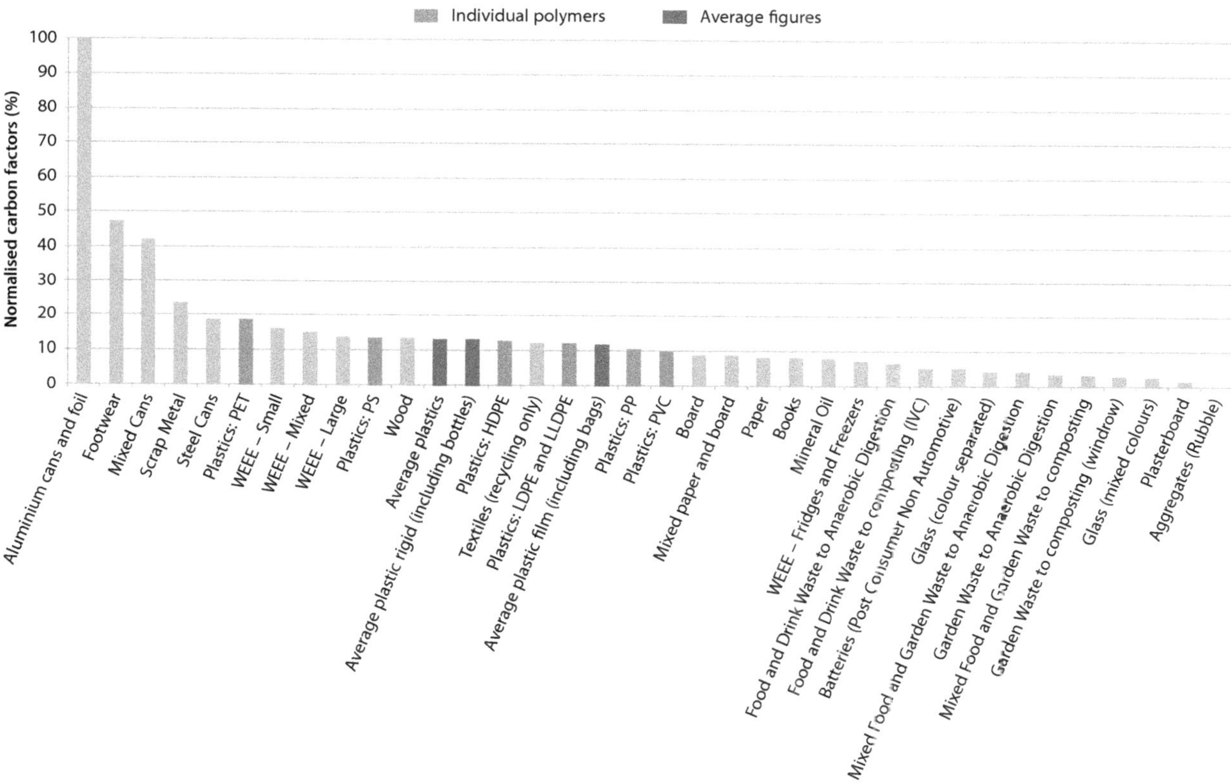

Source: Zero Waste Scotland (2017[71]), *Plastics to oil products*, http://bit.ly/2nAutov.

Annex G

International Waste Hierarchy according to the IPCC

Amassing LCA datasets and analysing them is a complex task and as such, conducting LCA studies is not regular or common practice amongst many plastics manufacturers, consumers and waste management professionals. The "Waste Hierarchy" provides a simplified system of ranking the best treatment options for waste products. There are several versions of the Waste Hierarchy which are used as guidance in different global regions, some of which are embedded in legislation, such as the European Waste Framework Directive. However, high-income countries do not usually include some of the lower levels below disposal which are shown in Figure F.1.

Figure G.1. **Waste hierarchy according to the Intergovernmental Panel on Climate Change**

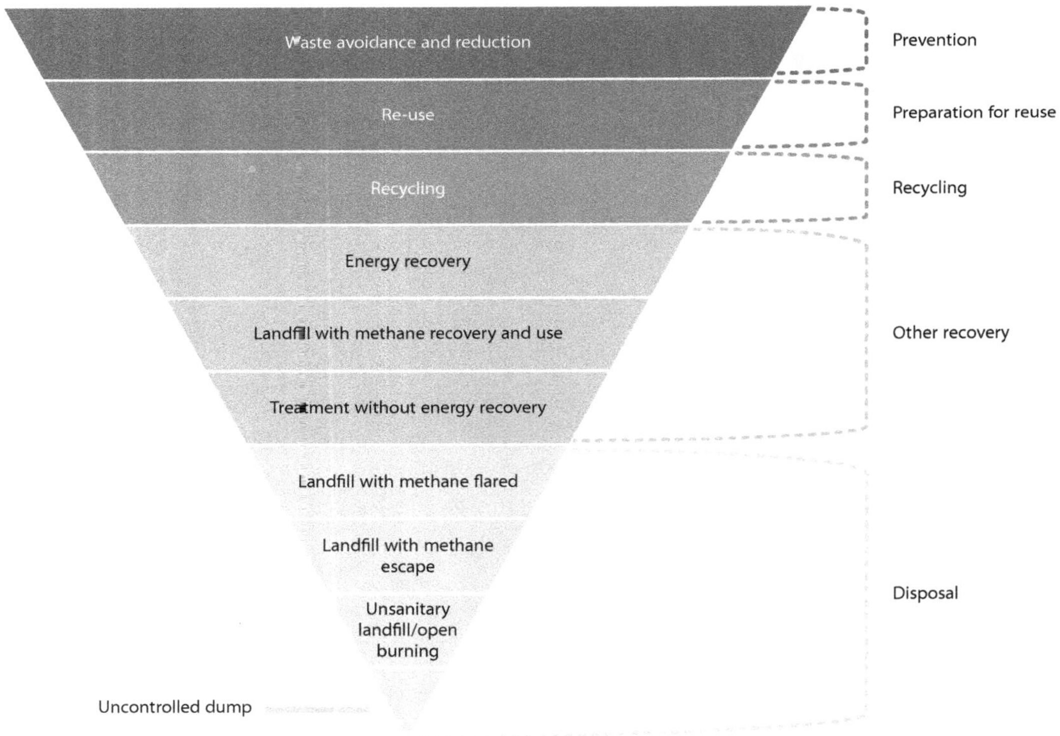

Annex H

Recycling targets

Table H.1. **UK recycling targets for specific packaging materials as of 2017**

	2014	2015	2016	2017	2018	2019	2020
	%	%	%	%	%	%	%
Glass	75	76	77	77	78	79	80
of which re-melt	65	66	67	67	67	67	67
Aluminium	46	49	52	55	58*	61*	64
Steel	73	74	75	76	79*	82*	85
Paper	69.5	69.5	69.5	69.5	71*	73*	75
Plastic	42	47	49*	51*	53	55	57
Wood	22	22	22	22	38*	43*	48
Total recycling	69.9	70.8	71.8	72.7	73.6*	74.5*	75.4
Total recovery	76	77	78	79	80*	81	82

Note: Figures marked with an "*" are in line with Defra consultation options, but are not yet confirmed

Table H.2. **EU recycling targets for specific packaging materials as of 2017**

	EU Directive target (%, in place since 2008)
Paper and board	60
Glass	60
Metal	50
Plastic	22.5
Wood	15
Total recycling and composting	55
Total energy recovery, recycling and composting	60

Table H.3. **Proposed EU recycling targets for specific packaging materials as of 2017**

	Proposed 2025 targets (%)	Proposed 2030 targets (%)
Paper and board	75	85
Glass	75	85
Ferrous metal	75	85
Aluminium	75	85
Plastic	55	
Wood	60	75
Total prepared for re-use and recycled	65	75

Note: These targets are currently being negotiated by the European Parliament, the Council and the European Commission and are therefore subject to change.

Annex I

Plastic waste disposal, recovery and recycling in Europe

Figure I.1. **Treatment of waste plastics in the EU (2006 to 2014)**

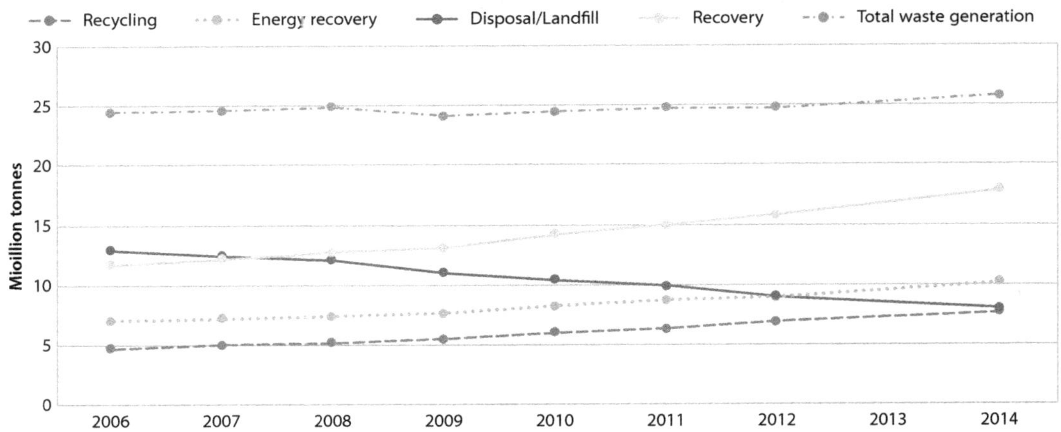

Source: Plastics Europe (2016[17]), *The impact of plastics on life cycle energy consumption and greenhouse gas emissions in Europe*, http://bit.ly/2hQw8s3.

Figure I.2. **Proportion of plastics recycled or treated by energy recovery in the EU (2014)**

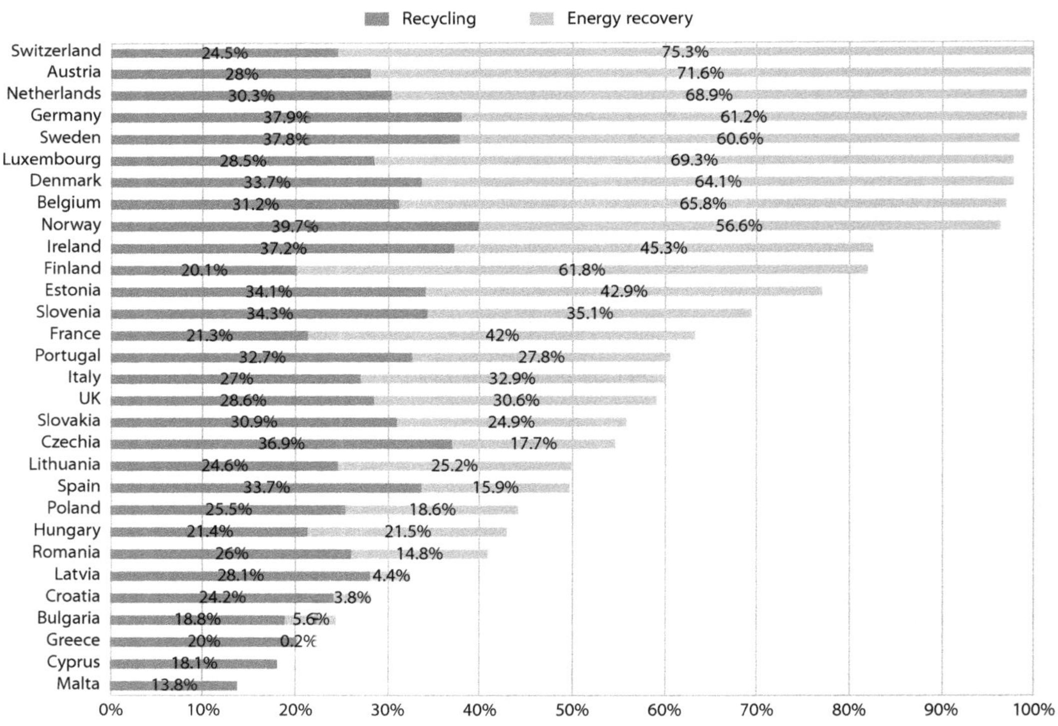

Annex J

Summary of polymer specific data from OECD questionnaire responses

Table J.1. **Australia: Waste stream sources of recyclate (tonnes) by polymer type (2015-16)**

Polymer	Municipal	Commercial and Industrial	Construction and demolition	Total
PET	64 200	8 400	0	72 600
PE-HD	63 900	31 000	2 500	97 500
PVC	1 600	2 700	900	5 300
PE-LD/LLD	2 800	66 000	200	69 000
PP	19 000	21 400	0	40 400
PS	4 100	4 100	1 000	9 200
PS-E	100	7 800	1 200	9 100
ABS/SAN	0	4 000	0	4 000
PU	0	6 200	0	6 200
Nylon	0	500	0	500
Other	5 500	4 200	2 900	12 600
Bioplastic	0	0	0	0
Synthetic rubbers	0	0	0	0
Unknown polymer	0	2 500	0	2 500
Totals	**161 300**	**158 900**	**8 700**	**328 900**

Table J.2. **United States: plastic recycling rate (2014)**

Polymer	Generation (thousand tonnes)	Recycling (thousand tonnes)	Recycling rate
PET	5 070	970	19.1%
HDPE	5 830	610	10.5%
PVC	840	Neg.	
LDPE/LLDPE	7 710	450	5.8%
PLA	60	Neg.	
PP	7 110	60	0.8%
PS	2 330	30	1.3%
Other resins	4 300	1 050	24.4%
Total Plastics in MSW	33 250	3 170	9.5%

Table J.3. **Japan: Plastic waste generation and mechanical recycling by polymer (2015)**

Type	Waste generation (million tons)	Mechanical recycling(million tonnes)	Recycling rate
PE	3	0.44	15%
PP	2.12	0.33	16%
PS	1.14	0.24	21%
PVC	0.78	0.19	24%
PET	0.6	0.51	85%
Other	1.5	0.34	23%
Total	9.15	2.05	

Annex K

Plastic sorters in the UK

Table K.1. **Plastic washing and flaking facilities in the UK**

Operator	Location	Capacity (tpa)	Description	Status
Jayplas (J & A Young)	Loughborough	unknown	Various waste plastics separation, pelletisation, extrusion, storage and export	Operational
	Loughborough			
	Loughborough			
	Corby			
	Birmingham			
	Grimsby			
	Worksop			
	Alfreton			
Viridor	Rochester	75 000	Sorting	Operational
Veolia	Rainham	50 000	Sorting	Operational
Monoworld	Rushden	100 000	Sorting, flaking and pelletisation	NEW washing and granulation
Greencircle Polymers	Livingstone	20 000	Sorting, flaking and pelletisation	Operational
Eco Plastics (Evolve Polymers)	Hemswell	150 000	Sorting, flaking and pelletisation	Flaking only
Biffa Polymers	Redcar	20 000	Sorting	Volatile
Closed loop	Dagenham	50 000	Sorting flaking and washing	Bust, but recently reopened in 2017 by Veolia following acquisition
Plastics Sorting Limited	Wales	24 000		Bust

Note: This is the reported capacity, these facilities are not required to report actual throughput, except for packaging, however the Environment Agency redacts these data from the national Packaging Waste Database.

Annex L

Summary of key data sources for recycled plastics

Table L.1. **Summary of key data sources for recycled plastics**

Dataset name
Precios materiales reciclados
Publisher
Anarpla
URL
http://anarpla.com/precios/precios-materiales-reciclados/
Polymers
HDPE, LDPE, PS, PP, ABS
Temporal scope
Monthly data in graphical form from January 2012 to April 2016 and monthly raw data available from February 2015 to December 2015
Geographical scope
Spain
Source of data and associated quality
Not known.
Any other comments
-

Dataset name
Comtrade
Publisher
United Nations
URL
https://comtrade.un.org/
Polymers
Waste polymers of ethylene, polymers of styrene, polymers of vinyl chloride, and “other” waste plastics
Temporal scope
Annual trade data from 1962 to the most recent year
Geographical scope
Global (close to 200 reporter countries/areas)

Source of data and associated quality

Countries/areas provide the United Nations Statistics Division (UNSD) with their annual international trade statistics data detailed by commodities/service categories and partner countries.

Similar to Eurostat data, Imports reported by one country do not coincide with exports reported by its trading partner. Differences are due to various factors including valuation (imports CIF, exports FOB), differences in inclusions/exclusions of particular commodities and timing.

Due to confidentiality, countries may not report some of its detailed trade.

Again recycled plastics prices are calculated by using the trade value of imports and exports divided by the tonnages to give a price per tonne. However, this is a rather crude estimate.

Any other comments

-

Dataset name

Comext

Publisher

Eurostat

URL

http://epp.eurostat.ec.europa.eu/newxtweb/

Polymers

Polymers of ethylene, polymers of styrene, polymers of vinyl chloride, polymers of propylene and "other" waste plastics

Temporal scope

Founded in 1953 but in terms of plastics and reliability of data, Eurostat state that from 2000 onwards there is a reliable EU-28 data base.

Annual and monthly data available.

Data are revised frequently according to national needs and practices. However, Member States must provide Eurostat with final detailed data at the latest by October following the reference year. This means that there should be complete data up until 2015 but 2016 data won't necessarily be complete until October of this year.

Geographical scope

European trade (internal and external with non-member states)

Source of data and associated quality

For the compilation of extra-EU trade statistics, the standard data source is the customs declaration submitted by businesses and, in some cases, by private individuals involved in an international transaction of goods with a non-EU country. The customs declaration may be in paper form – the Single Administrative Document (SAD) – but is most commonly in electronic format.

For intra-EU trade, any VAT-registered business that trades goods with other EU Member States is required to provide information on its transactions. The information is obtained directly by the national authority responsible for the collection of trade statistics. All businesses are legally required to provide information on their total sales and purchases to and from other EU countries on their VAT returns.

According to the EU legislation, revised data should be communicated to Eurostat within one month each time a revision occurs at national level.

The data shows quite significant differences between total imports and total exports. Asymmetries occur when the declaration of the importer in country A is not consistent with the declaration of the exporter in country B. Asymmetries come either from errors in reporting or from differences in the concepts and definitions applied by the partner countries. The most common causes of methodological asymmetries are the following:

- simplified product reporting: Where the EU legislation allows simplified codification of goods for certain transactions, some Member States apply the simplifications but others do not;
- confidentiality: It is possible that data are considered confidential by only one of the two partners.
- time lag: the same operation can be recorded under a different reference period because of transport times or processing delays;
- CIF/FOB valuation: imports are valued on a CIF basis and exports on a FOB basis. This causes a systematic asymmetry as the value of the imports should then be higher than the value of the mirror exports as they include extra transport costs;

- differences in methods and data used to estimate missing trade;
- different practices in the treatment of revisions;
- problems of currency conversion; and
- other methodological differences such as definition of partner country, definition of statistical territory, trade system (special or general).

Another possible source of asymmetries is the different application of thresholds for Intrastat declaration. The Intrastat legislation completely exempts traders with a low intra-EU trade value from any statistical reporting or allows the collection of simplified information. Member States nevertheless have to achieve the coverage rate required by the legislation: data must be collected directly from traders for 97 % of the dispatches in value and 95 % of the arrivals (93 % from 2014 onwards). The data not collected must be estimated but not at the most detailed level. The EU legislation states that estimates are to be allocated at least by chapter (HS2 codes) and partner Member States. Traders may also be given the possibility to report simplified information for small transactions below EUR 200. All these measures affect the data accuracy at the most detailed level, but full coverage of trade is still ensured. This amounts to a trade-off between data accuracy and the burden on businesses.

Trade data can be used to indicate recycled plastics prices by using the trade value of imports and exports divided by the tonnages to give a price per tonne. However, this is a rather crude estimate.

Any other comments

-

Dataset name

EUWID Markets and price trends

Publisher

EUWID Recycling and Waste Management

URL

www.euwid-recycling.com/markets.html

Polymers

Not known. Pay service only.

Temporal scope

Not known.

Geographical scope

Europe but focussed developments in Germany, the UK, France, Italy and Poland

Source of data and associated quality

They have a team of experienced business editors who research key market information at regular intervals through their network of industry contacts throughout Europe. They focus on the developments in Germany, the UK, France, Italy and Poland.

Any other comments

-

Dataset name

Recycling: Weighted average price of recycled materials

Publisher

Fostplus

URL

https://www.fostplus.be/en/about-fost-plus/numbers-and-charts

Polymers

HDPE and PET

Temporal scope

Graphical data (no raw data) from 2010-17

Geographical scope

Belgium

Source of data and associated quality

The charts show the weighted average value of contracts based on the standard specifications. The variations are determined by changes to contractual terms as a result of requests for tenders, revisions to the pricing formulas in the contracts and, to a lesser extent, fluctuations in the volumes collected on a monthly basis for each contract.

Any other comments

-

Dataset name

letsrecycle.com price indicators for plastics

Publisher

Let's Recycle

URL

www.letsrecycle.com/prices/plastics/

Polymers

Plastics bottles: Clear and light blue PET, Coloured PET, HDPE natural, HDPE mixed colour mixedPlastic films: UK PE Printed, UK PP Printed, UK Clear – Natural, Export 80:20, Export 90:10, Export, 95:5, Export 98:2

Temporal scope

2000/2001-present (although some data missing for plastic films)Monthly data

Geographical scope

UK

Source of data and associated quality

Data is collected via an email survey to merchants, reprocessors, exporters, local authorities and private sellers. Let's Recycle do not report the number of data sources/samples, but this is usually small (between 5 and 15) The method and sample size mean data is open to manipulation. Although data is collected monthly some businesses have long-term contracts for purchasing waste plastics which will mean that although value might fluctuate the pricing remains fixed over the period of the contract. Local authorities in the UK also have different collection and processing procedures for waste plastics and this may lead to problems standardising their data into the format used by Let's Recycle.

Any other comments

-

Dataset name

Plastics Information Europe Polymer Prices

Publisher

Plastics Information Europe

URL

https://pieweb.plasteurope.com/ (subscription: EUR 122/3months or EUR 360/12 months)

Polymers

PET, HDPE, LDPE, PP

Temporal scope

1984-present

Geographical scope

Western Europe and China, North America and Russia

Source of data and associated quality

Prices are based on information obtained by PIE from plastics converters, distributors, traders and producers. They are the outcome of an online survey (panel) and complemented and weighted by detailed telephone interviews. PIE has the plastics industry's largest network of contacts with more than 600 regular panel participants in Europe.
China, North America and Russia polymer prices are researched by local reporters and co-operation partners.
As a rule, PIE reports gross prices including delivery. They do not reflect any rebates, discounts or other net calculations, nor do they include VAT.

Any other comments

-

Dataset name

Historical Resin Pricing of Recycled Plastics

Publisher

Plastics News

URL

www.plasticsnews.com/resin/recycled-plastics/historical-pricing

Polymers

PET, HDPE, LDPE, PS, HMWHDPE, PVC, ABS, LLDPE, PP

Temporal scope

Dependant on polymer, 1989/91/92-present

Geographical scope

USA

Source of data and associated quality

Data is collected from "scores" of phone calls every week to officials at resin processors and producers, as well as consultants and analysts who follow the industry.

This data is thus open to manipulation, however Plastics News state that the ploys of producers and processors to increase or decrease pricing are usually fairly transparent and these contacts are removed as data sources and not contacted for future data collection.

Any other comments

-

Dataset name

CIF Ontario Price Sheet

Publisher

Reclay StewardEdge

URL

http://reclaystewardedge.com/resources/cif-ontario-price-sheet/

Polymers

PET, HDPE, LDPE, PS and PP

Temporal scope

Monthly price sheets from 2013-17

Geographical scope

Ontario, Canada

Source of data and associated quality

A combination of approximately 25 Ontario-based municipalities, end-users and brokers are email surveyed to collect and update recycled commodities pricing information. Initial contact is followed-up by more email and/or phone calls, as needed, to obtain and verify data. An "average" of the municipal data is calculated to determine current market prices. Where there are sufficient data points (five or more), the highest and lowest prices are dropped prior to calculating the average. Information from other contacts such as brokers, end-users and published sources are used as check points to verify the trends.

As with other "survey" data, this data is open to manipulation by producers and processors who might attempt to increase or decrease pricing by giving a false figure, however verification checks are made to reduce this.

Any other comments

-

Dataset name

Materials Pricing Report

Publisher

WRAP

URL

www.wrap.org.uk/content/materials-pricing-report

Polymers

Plastic bottles – Clear PET, Coloured PET, Mixed Polymers, Natural HDPE, Mixed HDPE LDPE film, carrier bags and mixed rigid plastics

Temporal scope

2008-present
Data collected weekly

Geographical scope

UK

Source of data and associated quality

Data collection is subcontracted to MRW magazine. To collect data on plastics prices they email a survey to merchants, reprocessors, exporters, local authorities and private sellers. WRAP do not report the number of data sources/samples, but this is usually small (between 5 and 15).

However, each segment of the industry has its own built-in agenda: Resin makers typically like to see prices going up; processors typically like to see prices going down. These agendas prompt some less-scrupulous industry operatives to try to push and pull the pricing chart in the direction they want it to go. The method and sample size mean data is open to manipulation.

Although data is collected weekly some businesses have long-term contracts for purchasing waste plastics which will mean that although value might fluctuate the pricing remains fixed over the period of the contract. Local authorities in the UK also have different collection and processing procedures for waste plastics and this may lead to problems standardising their data into the format used by WRAP.

Any other comments

-

Annex M

Exports of waste plastics

Table M.1. **Exports of waste plastics**

Country	2006	2007	2008	2009	2010	2011	2012	2013	2014	2015	Total (2006-15)
USA	1.06	1.39	1.61	2.04	2.06	2.15	2.05	1.94	2.18	2.05	20.48
Japan	1.30	1.52	1.51	1.49	1.64	1.63	1.67	1.68	1.67	1.61	17.24
Germany	0.75	0.85	0.77	1.45	1.42	1.46	1.51	1.32	1.45	1.38	13.81
United Kingdom	0.44	0.55	0.65	0.71	0.84	0.88	0.81	0.65	0.76	0.79	7.90
Mexico	0.35	0.42	0.44	0.37	0.41	0.44	0.52	0.52	0.86	0.45	5.21
France	0.38	0.39	0.39	0.45	0.48	0.50	0.51	0.45	0.48	0.47	4.98
Belgium	0.38	0.40	0.37	0.45	0.40	0.41	0.46	0.47	0.44	0.43	4.65
Netherlands	0.44	0.41	0.36	0.25	0.36	0.38	0.43	0.46	0.43	0.51	4.03
Rep. of Korea	0.30	0.32	0.29	0.31	0.20	0.16	0.18	0.18	0.19	0.19	2.54
Spain	0.09	0.11	0.11	0.17	0.22	0.19	0.24	0.23	0.33	0.33	2.34
Thailand	0.14	0.18	0.15	0.17	0.21	0.23	0.26	0.32	0.35	0.27	2.27
Canada	0.22	0.20	0.23	0.19	0.19	0.20	0.20	0.17	0.19	0.21	2.22
Italy	0.10	0.11	0.14	0.21	0.26	0.27	0.23	0.19	0.18	0.22	2.15
Australia	0.10	0.10	0.13	0.20	0.16	0.15	0.19	0.16	0.19	0.21	1.78
Malaysia	0.10	0.11	0.11	0.12	0.13	0.15	0.20	0.25	0.25	0.18	1.77
Other Asia	0.19	0.17	0.15	0.17	0.18	0.17	0.16	0.12	0.15	0.15	1.60
Denmark	0.04	0.05	0.25	0.13	0.49	0.08	0.09	0.07	0.08	0.07	1.52
Indonesia	0.04	0.06	0.05	0.05	0.12	0.17	0.20	0.23	0.19	0.15	1.47

Units: million tonnes. Year: 2015 (most recent full dataset available from UN Commtrade).

Note: Data excludes Hong Kong.

Source: adapted from UN Comtrade data (2017[84]), *Comtrade database*, http://bit.ly/2jL1FIk

Annex N

Imports of waste plastics

Table N.1. **Imports of waste plastics**

Country	2006	2007	2008	2009	2010	2011	2012	2013	2014	2015
China	5.86	6.91	7.07	7.33	8.01	8.38	8.88	7.88	8.25	7.35
Hong Kong	4.42	4.15	4.50	4.75	4.80	3.96	3.20	2.51	3.08	2.86
Netherlands	0.23	0.22	0.24	0.14	0.30	0.37	0.47	0.53	0.62	0.60
Germany	0.22	0.24	0.23	0.21	0.30	0.30	0.42	0.42	0.50	0.55
USA	0.56	0.42	0.41	0.36	0.38	0.34	0.36	0.37	0.42	0.39
Belgium	0.25	0.28	0.29	0.35	0.29	0.32	0.29	0.26	0.23	0.26
Malaysia	0.07	0.08	0.04	0.09	0.08	0.14	0.13	0.30	0.23	0.25
Canada	0.21	0.19	0.16	0.13	0.15	0.15	0.13	0.15	0.19	0.25
Austria	0.07	0.13	0.15	0.11	0.15	0.21	0.22	0.19	0.25	0.25
Other Asia	0.10	0.12	0.15	0.12	0.15	0.15	0.15	0.20	0.20	0.22
India	0.09	0.17	0.10	0.48	0.12	0.13	0.20	0.26	0.25	0.19
Sweden	0.02	0.08	0.09	0.14	0.30	0.26	0.13	0.21	0.15	0.18
Italy	0.19	0.20	0.16	0.12	0.14	0.15	0.14	0.13	0.16	0.15
Portugal	0.01	0.01	0.01	0.01	0.02	0.06	0.05	0.05	0.08	0.13
Czechia	0.03	0.04	0.05	0.05	0.06	0.09	0.11	0.12	0.13	0.13
France	0.07	0.07	0.08	0.06	0.10	0.11	0.11	0.11	0.11	0.12
Turkey	0.004	0.02	0.01	0.01	0.02	0.06	0.06	0.07	0.11	0.10
Indonesia	0.01	0.003	0.01	0.00	0.04	0.09	0.11	0.14	0.11	0.10

Units: million tonnes. Year: 2015 (most recent full dataset available from UN Commtrade).

Note: Includes all countries that imported over 100 000 tonnes of waste plastics in any one year since 2006. These countries account for 92% of global waste plastics imports in 2015.

Source: adapted from UN Comtrade data (2017[84]), *Comtrade database*, http://bit.ly/2jL1FIk.

Annex O

Time series analysis of prices paid for recycled plastics in China

Figure O.1. **Time-series analysis of prices paid for recycled acrylonitrile butadiene styrene (ABS) in China**

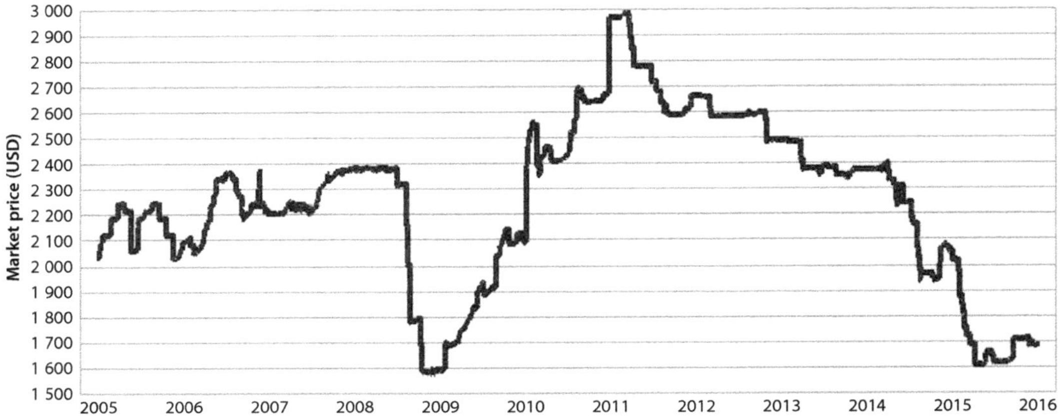

Note: Acrylonitrile butadiene styrene is commonly used in automotive applications as well as for making waste pipes, and for toys such as Lego

Source: OECD questionnaires.

Figure O.2. **Time-series analysis of prices paid for recycled HDPE in China**

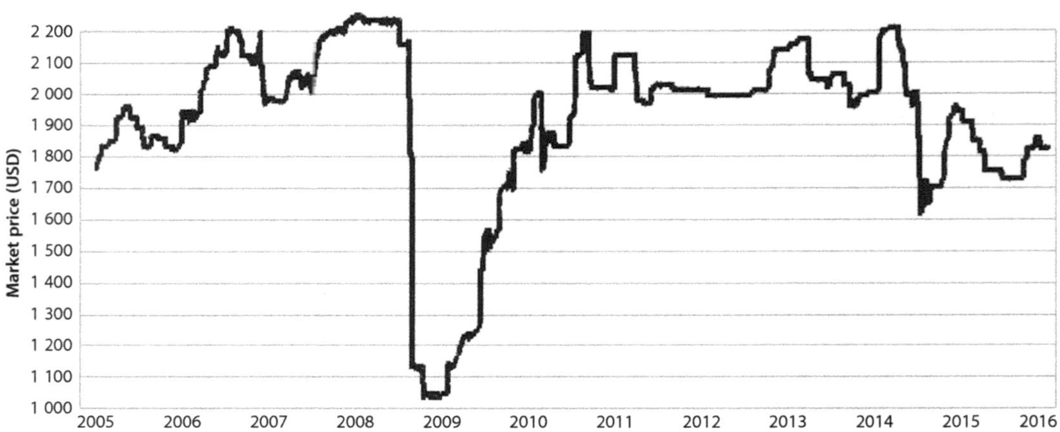

Source: OECD questionnaires.

Figure O.3. **Time-series analysis of prices paid for recycled LDPE in China**

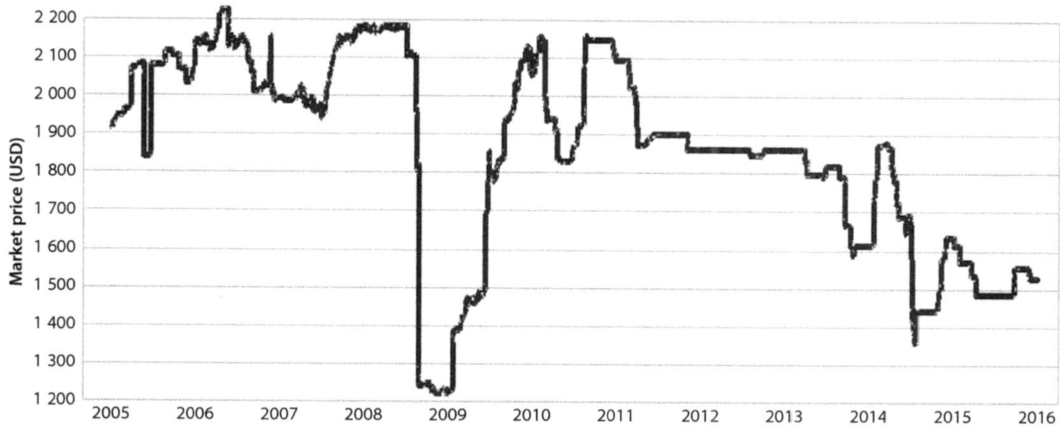

Source: OECD questionnaires.

Figure O.4. **Time-series analysis of prices paid for recycled polyamide (PA) in China**

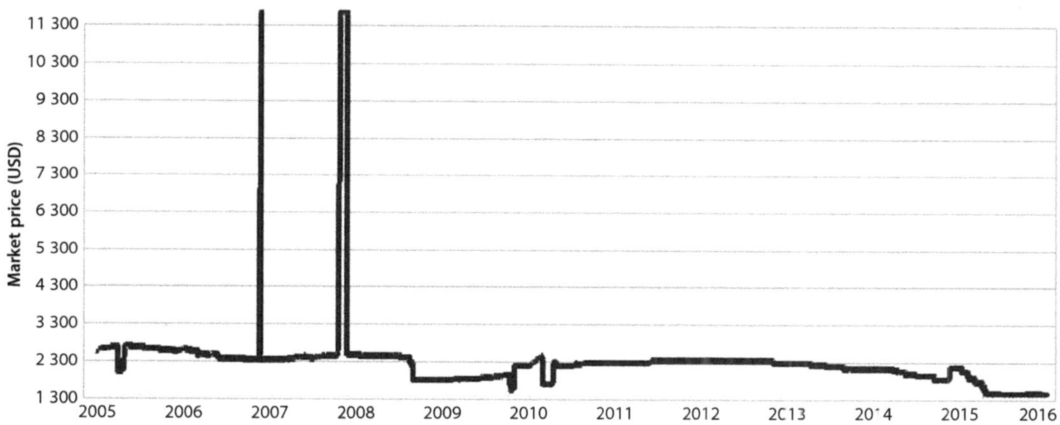

Source: OECD questionnaires.

Figure O.5. **Time-series analysis of prices paid for recycled PP in China**

Source: OECD questionnaires.

Figure O.6. **Time-series analysis of prices paid for recycled PS in China**

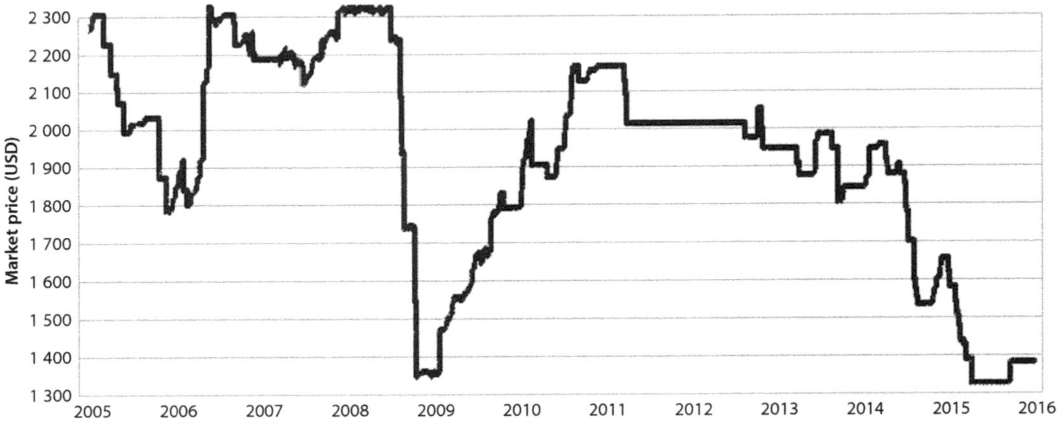

Source: OECD questionnaires.

Figure O.7. **Time-series analysis of prices paid for recycled PVC in China**

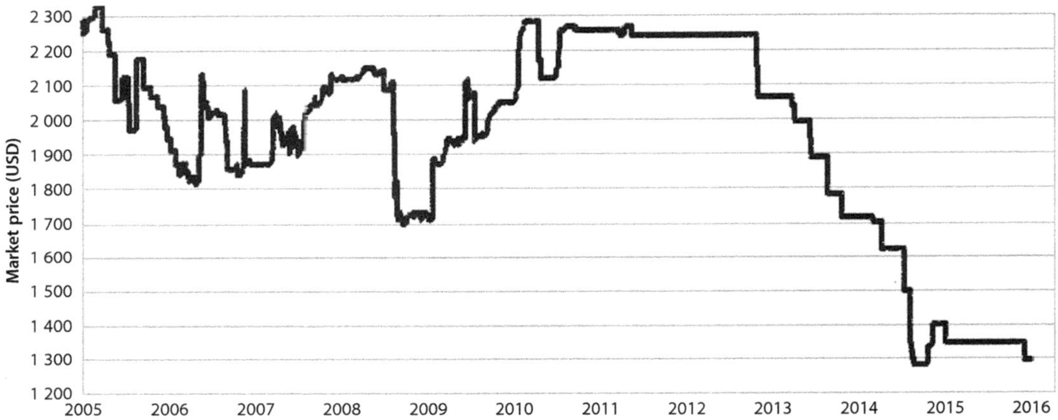

Source: OECD questionnaires.

Annex P

Overview of policies details provided by OECD questionnaire respondents

Table P.1. **Overview of policies details provided by OECD questionnaire respondents**

Policy	European Union	Netherlands	Austria	Canada	Switzerland	USA	Japan	China	Australia	Spain	Sweden	Belgium	Poland	Latvia	Estonia	Germany
Policies that improve quality (and quantity) of plastics waste collected for reprocessing																
Segregation of plastics for recycling	N			R							N					
Targets for plastic recycling	N			R							N					
Mandated source-segregated collection		N		R							N					
Landfill tax			N									N	N		N	N
Landfill ban of plastics			N	R							N					N
Reduced capacity of containers for collection of residual waste from households			N	R												
Pay as you throw (with higher residual charges)			N	R	N	R					R					
Convergence towards single system for recycling				R												
Ban on importing contaminated plastics								N								
EPR	N	N	N	R	N	R	N	N	N	N	N	N	N	N	N	N
Deposit collection schemes				R		R					N				N	N
Retailers obligated to collect end of life home appliances							N				N					
Penalties for designs known to hinder recycling																
Producers obligated to fund communications encouraging better waste management				R										N		N

Policy	European Union	Netherlands	Austria	Canada	Switzerland	USA	Japan	China	Australia	Spain	Sweden	Belgium	Poland	Latvia	Estonia	Germany
Mechanisms for increasing or improving manufacture using recycled plastics																
Guidelines for designing with recycled plastics		N														
Quality assurance guidance																N
Funding or projects to encourage symbiosis between companies to close the loop												R				
Subsidies for the development of technologies to support reprocessing				N			N									
Brokerage service to match supply with demand																
Policies and mechanisms that increase demand for recycled plastics																
"Eco" labels			N				N	N			N					N
Green public procurement		N		N		R	N			N	N	N		N		
Tools to help designers identify impacts and recycled variants	N					N						N				
Driving down costs of materials recycling						N										
Standards for manufacturing of certain items to require use recycled plastics						N										

Notes: OECD countries not included in the table: Chile, Czech Republic, Denmark, Finland, Greece, Hungary, Iceland, Ireland, Israel, Korea, Luxembourg, Mexico, New Zealand, Portugal, Slovak Republic, Slovenia, Turkey.

N: national level policy. **R**: regional or municipality level policy.

Annex Q

Detailed assessment of interventions

Table Q.1. **Summary of regulatory interventions**

No	Intervention	Barriers that could be addressed	Maturity	Comment	Feasibility	Comment	Impact	Comment
1	**Set statutory targets for recycling to drive supply of material, increase economies of scale, reduce costs and increase resilience.**	• Costs of collecting, sorting and processing waste plastics. • Limited resilience of the sector to market shocks.	H	Well-established in many member countries.	H	Demonstrated feasibility	H	Helps address many barriers and drive supply of recycled plastics.
2	**Ban plastics from landfill to drive supply of material and increase economies of scale, reduce costs and increase resilience.**	• Costs of collecting, sorting and processing waste plastics. • Limited resilience of the sector to market shocks.	M	Bans are established in a number of member countries.	M	Requires effective regulation and monitoring but is feasible.	M	Potential addresses several barriers, helping to drive supply of recycled plastics but materials may be diverted to other routes (e.g. energy from waste).
3	**Use Extended Producer Responsibility (EPR) regulation to drive supply of material and increase economies of scale, reduce costs and increase resilience.**	• Costs of collecting, sorting and processing waste plastics. • Limited resilience of the sector to market shocks.	H	Well-established in a number of member countries.	M	Some challenges associated with implementation but has demonstrated feasibility.	H	Helps address several barriers and drive up supply of recycled plastics.
4	**Standardise waste collection systems to increase economies of scale and reduce costs.**	• Costs of collecting, sorting and processing waste plastics. • Plastics contaminated and mixed with other materials.	M	Established in a number of member countries.	M	Has demonstrated feasibility but there are some challenges associated with creating uniform systems (e.g. England).	M	Helps address several barriers and drive up supply of recycled plastics.
5	**Mandate requirement for recycled content to create demand.**	• Lack of differentiated demand for recycled plastics.	L	No examples identified of mandatory requirements for recycled content.	M	Will require supply chain engagement and may meet resistance.	H	Only addresses one barrier but it is key one. Could have a strong demand side impact

No	Intervention	Barriers that could be addressed	Maturity	Comment	Feasibility	Comment	Impact	Comment
6	**Use public sector procurement policies to create demand for recycled content.**	• Lack of differentiated demand for recycled plastics.	M	"Green procurement" established in a number of member countries but, to-date, limited focus on plastics.	H	Considered to have good feasibility given that it is government-driven.	M/H	Could have moderate to high impact in driving demand for supply of recycled content (but less than mandating recycled content for manufacturers – above).
7	**Introduce mandatory data reporting mechanisms for plastics recycling.**	• Poor data on the plastics recycling industry.	M	Applied in principle in, for example, the EU but provides poor quality data.	H	Considered to have good feasibility given that it is government-driven.	M	Could help stimulate the market and encourage new market entrants.
8	**Ban or reduce problematic additives in primary plastics.**	• Problematic additives.	L	Intervention has not been applied in the context of recycled plastics.	M	Potentially feasible, but will require co-ordinated action and support from supply chain.	M	Has potential to address problematic additives issue, although legacy issues will still exist.
9	**Mandate labelling for biodegradable plastics and improve associated standards.**	• Bio-degradable plastics mixing with other plastics.	L	Not yet established.	M	Will require co-ordinated action and support from supply chain.	M	Could help address this key barrier but unlikely to be total solution.
10	**Set targets (including using EPR) for recycling thermosets to drive supply.**	• Limited collection schemes and treatment technologies for thermosets.	L	Not yet established	M	Considered to have good feasibility but will require supply chain engagement	M	Has potential to have significant effect on driving supply of recycled thermoset plastics.
11	**Ban or reduce hazardous additives from primary plastics.**	• Hazardous additives.	M	Some specific examples of its application exist.	M	Will require co-ordinated action and support from supply chain.	M	Could address hazardous additives, although legacy issues will still exist.
12	**Ban plastics from energy from waste.**	• Competition between recycling and energy from waste.	L	No identified examples	L/M	Potentially feasible but likely to be resisted strongly by energy from waste sector.	M	If combined with other measures (e.g. landfill bans or taxes), this intervention could increase supply of recycled plastics.
13	**Ensure regulation is proportionate and clarify end-of-waste requirements.**	• Regulatory burdens of materials classified as waste.	M	End of Waste status in the EU is an example of this intervention.	M	Has demonstrated feasibility where appropriate regulatory framework in place.	M	Only addresses one barrier so has is thought to have a relatively low impact.
14	**Enforcement action to reduce illegal dumping, particularly in low and middle income countries where dumping is common place.**	• Uncontrolled dumping and burning of municipal wastes.	M	Well-established in most member countries but less so in low and middle income countries.	M	Well demonstrated but requires effective legislative framework and resources for enforcement.	H	Essential requirement of properly functioning markets for recycled plastics.

No	Intervention	Barriers that could be addressed	Maturity	Comment	Feasibility	Comment	Impact	Comment
15	**Enforcement action to reduce illegal waste trafficking.**	• Illegal trafficking in waste plastics.	M	International agreements are well-established but are also continuing to evolve (e.g. China's National Sword).	M	Well demonstrated but international co-operation and action is essential for implementation.	H	Essential requirement of properly functioning markets for recycled plastics.
16	**Regulation and enforcement to ensure consistent environmental standards in global markets**	• Concerns over environmental standards for recycling in emerging markets.	M	Well-established in most member countries but less so in low and middle income countries.	M	Well demonstrated but international co-operation and action is also essential.	M	Likely to help markets for recycled plastics to function effectively.
17	**Mandate sellers to establish and audit end-destinations for environmental standards.**	• Concerns over environmental standards for recycling in emerging markets.	L	This is essentially a mandatory "duty of care" but has not yet been applied extensively to plastics.	L	Implementing this type of approach would require an international approach, which could prove very challenging.	M	Likely to help markets for recycled plastics to function effectively.
18	**Obligate monomer manufacturers to buy back recycled plastics**	• Lack of differentiated demand for recycled plastics.	L	Not applied to date	L	Likely to be met with string resistance by plastics sector	M	Impact is uncertain as it will depend upon the targets that are set.

Table Q.2. **Summary of economic interventions**

No	Intervention	Barriers that could be addressed	Maturity	Comment	Feasibility	Comment	Impact	Comment
1	**Mobilise investment for developing collection, sorting and processing systems, particularly in low income contexts.**	• Costs of collecting, sorting and processing waste plastics. • Collection systems for wastes not available for a substantial proportion of the global population.	M	A well-demonstrated intervention but investment in the sector is currently relatively low Financing mechanisms for waste systems in low income countries, in particular, are not well-established.	M	Feasible but challenging, requiring widespread partnership between government and private sector.	H	Investment in collection, sorting and reprocessing infrastructure is a key requirement for properly functioning markets for recycled plastics.

No	Intervention	Barriers that could be addressed	Maturity	Comment	Feasibility	Comment	Impact	Comment
2	**Use financial market mechanisms to increase the resilience of the market to fluctuations in prices** (e.g. **futures markets or centrally managed risk funds).**	• Limited resilience of the sector to market shocks.	L	The use of market-based financial instruments for managing risk in markets for recycled plastics has had very limited application to-date.	M	In principal, these mechanisms are feasible but the small number of examples have encountered some challenges.	H	Effect unknown but these mechanisms could potentially make a significant difference in addressing the sector's vulnerability, a key barrier.
3	**Support development of domestic reprocessing capacity to reduce reliance on global markets.**	• Global markets dominated by China.	M	There has been some investment in Europe and North America around this issue but the activity has been largely focused on collection and sorting systems, rather than domestic recycling capacity.	M/H	Feasible but will require action and investment by both national governments and industry.	M/H	This has the potential to significantly increase the sector's resilience.
4	**Use taxes or trading mechanisms to internalise the externalities associated with primary plastics. This will support the price of recycled plastics.**	• Lack of differentiated demand for recycled plastics.	L	Limited implementation to-date	L/M	These mechanisms are feasible but will require co-ordinate action by all stakeholders.	H	This has the potential to significantly increase the value of recycled plastics relative to primary plastics.
5	**Tax additives that cause detrimental effects on recycled plastics (including degradability enhancers).**	• Problematic additives.	L	An approach that has not yet been applied.	L	Very difficult approach to implement given the complexity and confidentiality around additive use. Also likely to be met with resistance.	M	If implemented successfully this has the potential to significantly disincentivise the use of problematic additives and could address this issue.
6	**Incentivise recycling over energy from waste by introducing a tax to reflect the relative environmental burden/ benefit.**	• Competition between recycling and energy from waste.	L	Not applied to-date.	M	Likely to be met with considerable resistance from the energy from waste sector.	L/M	Using a differentiated tax to reflect the relative impact, has potential to disincentivise energy from waste for plastics and increase supply of recycled plastics in some contexts.
7	**Introduce tax incentives to encourage use of recycled plastics** (e.g. **VAT exemptions).**	• Lack of differentiated demand for recycled plastics.	L	No known examples.	L/M	Likely to require concerted action from government to implement.	M	Likely to increase demand for recycled content but impact uncertain.
8	**Charge waste producers for collection and disposal of non-recyclable waste.**	• Costs of collecting, sorting and processing waste plastics.	M	Established in a number of member countries.	M	Feasible but likely to meet some pollical and public resistance	M	Likely to drive the supply of recycled plastics.

Table Q.3. **Summary of technology interventions**

No	Intervention	Barriers that could be addressed	Maturity	Comment	Feasibility	Comment	Impact	Comment
1	**Support development of better and more cost-effective technologies for collecting, transporting and sorting waste plastics.**	• Costs of collecting, sorting and processing waste plastics.	M	There has been considerable technology development over recent years but further opportunities exist.	M	Feasible but largely dependent upon technology break-throughs and government/funding support.	H	Technology innovation could radically address one of the main barriers to effective markets for recycled plastics.
2	**Support the development and demonstration of commercially viable technologies for mixed and/or low value plastics.**	• Plastics contaminated and mixed with other materials	L	There is considerable scope for further developing and demonstrating technologies for treating mixed and/or low value plastics.	M	Feasible but largely dependent upon tech-nology break-throughs and government/fund-ing support.	H	Technology innovation could radically address one of the main barriers to effective markets for recycled plastics.
3	**Develop alternatives to problematic and hazardous additives.**	• Problematic additives.	L	Beginning to get more attention but this has not been a key focus to-date.	M	Feasible but largely dependent upon research developments and government/ funding support.	M	Could be key in addressing this issue and help drive supply and demand for some polymers/products.
4	**Develop technologies that can identify or track problematic and hazardous additives so that they can be eliminated from recycled plastics.**	• Problematic additives.	L	Not yet widely applied.	M	Feasible but largely dependent upon research developments and government/ funding support.	M	Could be key in addressing this issue and help drive supply and demand for some polymers/products.
5	**Develop purifying and stabilising technologies that can overcome the physical effects of problematic additives in recycled plastics.**	• Problematic additives.	L	Not yet widely applied.	M	Feasible but largely dependent upon research developments and government/ funding support.	M	Could be key in addressing this issue and help drive supply and demand for some polymers/products.
6	**Develop technologies for identifying biodegradable plastics**	• Biodegradable plastics mixing with other plastics.	L/M	Existing technologies can detect biodegradable plastics but they are not extensively used for this purpose.	M	Technically feasible but potentially costly.	M	Has good potential to address this barrier.
7	**Develop purifying and stabilising technologies that can overcome the physical effects of biodegradable plastics in waste plastics streams.**	• Biodegradable plastics mixing with other plastics.	L	It is not thought that this approach has been applied or developed to-date.	L	Feasibility uncertain and largely dependent upon research devel-opments and govern-ment/funding support.	L/M	Has some potential to address this barrier but limited effect on wider market issues.
8	**Develop and demonstrate effective systems for collecting and recycling thermosets**	• Limited collection schemes and treatment technologies for thermosets.	L/M	Some systems and technologies exist but these are not widely applied.	M	Feasible but requires stakeholder support and investment.	M	Has potential to have significant effect on driving supply of recycled thermoset plastics.

Table Q.4. **Summary of data and information interventions**

No	Intervention	Barriers that could be addressed	Maturity	Comment	Feasibility	Comment	Impact	Comment
1	**Raise public awareness to create demand for plastics recycling, reduce contamination, and to reduce littering and dumping.**	• Costs of collecting, sorting and processing waste plastics. • Collection systems for wastes not available for a substantial proportion of the global population. • Plastics contaminated and mixed with other materials. • Limitod oolloction cohomoc and treatment technologies for thermosets. • Uncontrolled dumping and burning of municipal wastes.	M/H	Public awareness has increased but there is scope to do more.	H	There are well-established methods for raising public awareness.	H	Could help address many barriers
2	**Share best practice on all aspects of the collection, sorting and reprocessing supply chain.**	• Costs of collecting, sorting and processing waste plastics. • Collection systems for wastes not available for a substantial proportion of the global population. • Plastics contaminated and mixed with other materials.	M	This approach is well-established but there is considered to be scope to do more.	H	Sharing best practice is highly feasible.	H	This could address many barriers
3	**Develop and share market information to allow actors to expand into new markets. A more globalised market will reduce reliance on a single actor.**	• Poor data on the plastics recycling industry. • Global markets dominated by China. • Limited resilience of the sector to market shocks.	L	Data and information for the sector is poor.	H	Feasible and relatively low cost compared to infrastructure investment but will require co-ordinated action.	M/H	Could help stimulate the market and address several barriers.
4	**Enhance supply chain awareness of problematic additives so that the impact on markets for recycled plastics is understood.**	• Problematic additives.	L/M	Relatively low supply awareness of the issue around additives.	M	Feasible bu.t will require co-ordinated action throughout the supply chain.	M	Has potential to help address the issue of problematic additives.
5	**Provide information to designers and manufacturers to encourage use of recycled content.**	• Lack of differentiated demand for recycled plastics.	M	Has been applied for specific applications (e.g. PET bottles) but scope to do more.	H	Demonstrated feasibility. Requires supply chain support.	H	Could continue to help address a key demand-side barrier.

No	Intervention	Barriers that could be addressed	Maturity	Comment	Feasibility	Comment	Impact	Comment
6	**Provide information to consumers to encourage purchase of products using recycled content and drive demand.**	• Lack of differentiated demand for recycled plastics.	M	Public awareness has increased but there is scope to do more.	H	There are well-established methods for raising public awareness.	M/H	Could help address this key demand-side barrier.
7	**Provide clear labelling and information for biodegradable plastics to encourage appropriate management by consumers.**	• Biodegradable plastics mixing with other plastics.	M	Established but scope for wider application and improvement.	H	Labelling of biodegradable plastics highly feasible.	M	Could help address this key supply-side barrier for this material.
8	**Reduce uncertainty over the health effects of hazardous additives.**	• Hazardous additives	M	An issue that has been assessed over many years but concerns still exist.	M	Feasible dependent upon appropriate government leadership and research efforts.	M	Could help address this key barrier.
9	**Encourage openness about standards and provide information on end-destinations.**	• Concerns over environmental standards for recycling in emerging markets.	L/M	Some efforts on end-destinations has been done but scope to do more.	M	Requires strong supply chain co-operation.	M	Could help address this key barrier.

Table Q.5. **Summary of voluntary interventions**

No	Intervention	Barriers that could be addressed	Maturity	Comment	Feasibility	Comment	Impact	Comment
1	**Create voluntary standards for collection, sorting and reprocessing.**	• Costs of collecting, sorting and processing waste plastics.	M	Some examples exist but could be improved and extended for plastics.	M	Feasible but co-ordinated action needed.	M	Could help address this key barrier.
2	**Work with supply chain to encourage use of recycled content.**	• Lack of differentiated demand for recycled plastics.	M	Applied for some applications (e.g. PIRAP).	H	Demonstrated feasibility. Requires supply chain support.	H	Could continue to help address a key demand-side barrier.
3	**Industry-led initiative to standardise polymers and additives, and improve information on additives.**	• Separating polymers from other materials, other polymers and contamination.	M	Some efforts underway wat to address this issue (e.g. Global Plastics Protocol)	M	Feasible but requires concerted action from a wide-range of stakeholders.	M/H	Could help address this key barrier.
4	**Industry-led phase out of problematic and hazardous additives from primary plastics.**	• Problematic additives.	M	Some examples of this intervention exist (e.g. lead-based fire retardants)	M	Feasible but requires co-ordinated cation from supply chain.	M	Could help address key barrier

No	Intervention	Barriers that could be addressed	Maturity	Comment	Feasibility	Comment	Impact	Comment
5	**Develop effective voluntary standards for recycling sector to limit need for regulation.**	• Regulatory burdens of materials classified as waste.	L	Limited application in the context of materials classified as waste (normally regulatory rather than voluntary).	M	Feasible but requires co-ordinated action from supply chain stakeholders.	M	Could help address this key barrier.
6	**Industry-led initiatives to crack down on waste crime.**	• Illegal trafficking in waste plastics.	L/M	Some examples of efforts have been made by industry but not widespread.	M	Feasible but requires co-ordinated action from industry.	H	Essential requirement of properly functioning markets for recycled plastics.
7	**Industry-led initiative to ensure consistent environmental standards in global markets.**	• Concerns over environmental standards for recycling in emerging markets	L	Limited industry-action taken to-date on this issue.	L	Implementing this type of approach would require an international approach, which could prove very challenging.	M	Likely to help markets for secondary plastics to function effectively.

Annex R

Examples of innovation in plastics

Table R.1. **Ellen MacArthur Foundation innovation examples**

Innovation	Description	Current state
Removing additives	Separating additives from recovered polymers to increase recyclate purity	Lab stage: Some technologies exist but with limited application
Reversible adhesives	Recycling multi-material packaging by designing "reversible" adhesives that allow for triggered separation of different material layers	Conceptual stage: Innovation needed to develop cost-competitive adhesive
Super-polymer	Finding a super-polymer that combines functionality and cost with superior after-use properties	Conceptual stage: Innovation needed to develop cost-competitive polymer with desired functional and after-use properties
Depolymerisation	Recycling plastics to monomer feedstock (building blocks) for virgin-quality polymers	Lab stage: Proven technically possible for polyolefins Limited adoption: Large-scale adoption of depolymerisation for PET hindered by processing costs
Chemical markets	Sorting plastics by using dye, ink or other additive markers detectable by automated sorting technology	Pilot stage: Food-grade markers available but unproven under commercial operating conditions
Near infrared	Sorting plastics by using automated optical sorting technology to distinguish polymer types	Fragmented adoption: Large-scale adoption limited by capex demands
Benign in marine environments	Design plastics that are less harmful to marine environments in case of leakage	Lab stage: Marine degradable plastics theoretically freshwater degradable. One certified product – impact of large-scale adoption to be proven
Benign in freshwater	Design plastics that are less harmful to freshwater environments in case of leakage	Lab stage: Marine degradable plastics theoretically freshwater degradable. One certified product – impact of large-scale adoption to be proven
GHG-based	Sourcing plastics from carbon in greenhouse gases released by industrial or waste management processes	Pilot stage: CO_2-based proven cost competitive in pilots; methane-based being scaled up to commercial volumes
Bio-based	Sourcing plastics from carbon in biomass	Limited adoption: Large-scale adoption hindered by limited economies of scale and sophistication of global supply chains

Source: EMF (2016[31]), *The New Plastics Economy*, http://bit.ly/2jgkkfK.

References

Anderson, J. (2015), "ATH use in flame retardants: An overview of the industry and growth in Asia", *Roskill*, https://www.metalbulletin.com/events/download.ashx/document/speaker/8449/a0ID000000X0j5MMAR/Presentation (accessed on 27 March 2018). [83]

Birnbaum, L. and D. Staskal (2004), "Brominated Flame Retardants: Cause for Concern?", http://dx.doi.org/10.1289/ehp.6559. [105]

C&EN (2015), *Plasticizers Makers Want a Piece of the Phthalates Pie*, The American Chemical Society, https://cen.acs.org/articles/93/i25/Plasticizer-Makers-Want-Piece-Phthalates.html (accessed on 27 March 2018). [76]

Ceresana (2016), "Market Study: Flame retardants", http://bit.ly/2y889cj (accessed on 27 March 2018). [104]

COWI (2013), "Hazardous substances in plastics materials", www.miljodirektoratet.no/old/klif/publikasjoner/3017/ta3017.pdf (accessed on 26 March 2018). [13]

Defra (2012), "England Carbon Metric", http://bit.ly/2vm94c3 (accessed on 29 March 2018). [111]

EMF (2016), "The New Plastics Economy", https://www.ellenmacarthurfoundation.org/assets/downloads/EllenMacArthurFoundation_TheNewPlasticsEconomy_15-3-16.pdf (accessed on 26 March 2018). [34]

Geyer, R., J. Jambeck and K. Law (2017), "Production, use, and fate of all plastics ever made", *Science Advances*, Vol. 3/7, p. e1700782, http://dx.doi.org/10.1126/sciadv.1700782. [1]

IHS (2015), *Plasticizers*, https://ihsmarkit.com/products/plasticizers-chemical-economics-handbook.html (accessed on 27 March 2018). [77]

Institute for Bioplastics and Biocomposites (2017), "Biopolymers", https://www.ifbb-hannover.de/files/IfBB/downloads/faltblaetter_broschueren/Biopolymers-Facts-Statistics_2017.pdf (accessed on 26 March 2018). [21]

International Labour Office (2012), *Chemical Processing*, www.ilocis.org/documents/chpt77e.htm (accessed on 27 March 2018). [103]

ISRI (2017), "ISRI Position on the Use of Degradable Additives in Plastic Packaging", www.isri.org/docs/default-source/policy-position-statements/use-of-degradable-additives-in-plastic-packaging.pdf (accessed on 27 March 2018). [87]

ISRI (2017), "Statement of the Institute of Scrap Recycling Industries", www.isri.org/docs/default-source/default-document-library/isri-comments-to-the-wto-re-notification-gtbtnchn1211-august-18-2017.pdf?sfvrsn=2 (accessed on 26 March 2018). [61]

Mashek, B. (2016), "Bioplastics", *Plastics Market Watch*, www.plasticsindustry.org/sites/plastics.dev/files/2016PMWBioplasticsIA.pdf (accessed on 28 March 2018). [110]

Merchant Research & Consulting (2013), *World BPA Production Grew by Over 372,000 Tonnes in 2012*, https://mcgroup.co.uk/news/20131108/bpa-production-grew-372000-tonnes.html (accessed on 27 March 2018). [85]

Michaud, J., L. Farrant and O. Jan (2010), "Environmental benefits of recycling", *WRAP*, www.wrap.org.uk/sites/files/wrap/Environmental_benefits_of_recycling_2010_update.3b174d59.8816.pdf (accessed on 26 March 2018). [19]

Phantom Plastics((n.d.)), *Functional Fillers and Specialty Minerals for Plastics*, http://phantomplastics.com/functional-fillers/ (accessed on 27 March 2018). [80]

Plastics Europe (2016), "Plastics – the Facts 2017: An analysis of European plastics production, demand and waste data", https://www.plasticseurope.org/application/files/5715/1717/4180/Plastics_the_facts_2017_FINAL_for_website_one_page.pdf (accessed on 26 March 2018). [17]

Rutland Plastics((n.d.)), *Plastics Additives- Flame Retardants*, www.rutlandplastics.co.uk/plastics-additives-intro/plastics-additives-fr/ (accessed on 27 March 2018). [82]

Segev, O., A. Kushmaro and A. Brenner (2009), "Environmental Impact of Flame Retardants (Persistence and Biodegradability)", *Int. J. Environ. Res. Public Health International Journal of Environmental Research and Public Health Int. J. Environ. Res. Public Health*, Vol. 6/6, pp. 478-491, http://dx.doi.org/10.3390/ijerph6020478. [81]

SPI (2015), "Compatibilizers: Creating New Opportunity for Mixed Plastics", www.plasticsindustry.org/sites/plastics.dev/files/Compatibilizers%20Whitepaper%20%28Version%201.0%29_0.pdf (accessed on 27 March 2018). [86]

Thompson, R. et al. (2009), "Plastics, the environment and human health: current consensus and future trends", *Philosophical Transactions of the Royal Society B: Biological Sciences*, Vol. 364/1526, p. 2153, http://dx.doi.org/10.1098/RSTB.2009.0053. [84]

UN (2017), *Comtrade Database*, https://comtrade.un.org/ (accessed on 26 March 2018). [56]

UNEP (2015), "Biodegradable plastics and marine litter: misconceptions, concerns and impacts on marine environments", https://wedocs.unep.org/bitstream/handle/20.500.11822/7468/-Biodegradable_Plastics_and_Marine_Litter_Misconceptions,_concerns_and_impacts_on_marine_environments-2015BiodegradablePlasticsAndMarineLitter.pdf.pdf?sequence=3&isAllowed=y (accessed on 27 March 2018). [108]

Villanueva, A. and P. Eder (2014), "End-of-waste criteria for waste plastic for conversion", *European Commission: JRC Technical Reports*, http://publications.jrc.ec.europa.eu/repository/bitstream/111111111/33010/1/2014-jrc91637%20.pdf (accessed on 26 March 2018). [14]

Vinyl Plus (2014), "The European PVC industry's experience in replacing lead and cadmium-based stabilisers", www.stabilisers.eu/wp-content/uploads/2015/11/VinylPlus_Contribution-Cefic_Eu-Industry.pdf (accessed on 27 March 2018). [79]

Wong, C. (2009), "A Study of Plastic Recycling Supply Chain", https://www.ciltuk.org.uk/portals/0/documents/pd/seedcornwong.pdf (accessed on 26 March 2018). [91]

Zero Waste Scotland (2017), *Scottish Materials Brokerage Service*, www.zerowastescotland.org.uk/brokerage (accessed on 26 March 2018). [73]

ORGANISATION FOR ECONOMIC CO-OPERATION AND DEVELOPMENT

The OECD is a unique forum where governments work together to address the economic, social and environmental challenges of globalisation. The OECD is also at the forefront of efforts to understand and to help governments respond to new developments and concerns, such as corporate governance, the information economy and the challenges of an ageing population. The Organisation provides a setting where governments can compare policy experiences, seek answers to common problems, identify good practice and work to co-ordinate domestic and international policies.

The OECD member countries are: Australia, Austria, Belgium, Canada, Chile, the Czech Republic, Denmark, Estonia, Finland, France, Germany, Greece, Hungary, Iceland, Ireland, Israel, Italy, Japan, Korea, Latvia, Luxembourg, Mexico, the Netherlands, New Zealand, Norway, Poland, Portugal, the Slovak Republic, Slovenia, Spain, Sweden, Switzerland, Turkey, the United Kingdom and the United States. The European Union takes part in the work of the OECD.

OECD Publishing disseminates widely the results of the Organisation's statistics gathering and research on economic, social and environmental issues, as well as the conventions, guidelines and standards agreed by its members.

OECD PUBLISHING, 2, rue André-Pascal, 75775 PARIS CEDEX 16
(97 2018 07 1 P) ISBN 978-92-64-30100-9 – 2018

www.ingramcontent.com/pod-product-compliance
Lightning Source LLC
Chambersburg PA
CBHW061216240926
51846CB00006B/1240
9789264301009